FIREFLIES
ON THE BEDPOST

MARK EVANS

Fireflies On The Bedpost

**DON'T LET THE MESS IN YOUR HEAD RUIN
THE BEAUTY OF YOUR TOMORROW.**

Mark Evans

ISBN: 1539783936
ISBN 13: 9781539783930
Library of Congress Control Number: 2016919283
CreateSpace Independent Publishing Platform
North Charleston, South Carolina

Don't let the mess in your head ruin the beauty of your tomorrow.
—*Mark*

"Once upon a time I had anxious thoughts, but I found freedom."
—*StellB.*

"I was selfish and controlling, but I found freedom." *Olivia P.*

"I was frustrated and wanting more, but I found freedom." *Lewy C.*

"I was in a dark place feeling lost and confused, but I found freedom." *Laura A.*

"I was selfish, but I found freedom." *Phil A.*

"I was insecure and tormented, but I found freedom." *Robbyn E.*

"I was confused and angry, but I found freedom." *Jason P.*

"I was tormented and trapped, but I found freedom." *Jennifer R.*

"I was on the fence feeling ostracized, but I found freedom." *Joe K.*

"I was always hiding my hurt and worry behind my smile, but I found freedom." *Cassidy T.*

"I was forsaken, but I found freedom." *Mike S.*

"I was suppressed, but I found freedom." *Sarah W.*

"I was imperfect, but I found freedom." *Shelia R.*

"I was totally deceived, but I found freedom." *Matt C.*

"I was alone, but I found freedom." *Dustin K.*

"I was just plain ol' lost, but I found freedom." *Chris R.*

"I was lustful and fearful, but I found freedom." *Jeff C.*

"I was worthless and beaten down not understanding how God loved me, but I found freedom." *Windy D.*

"I was a broken mess, but I found freedom." *Reggie C.*

"I was suicidal, but I found freedom." *Beth R.*

"I was in a deep depression, but I found freedom." *Chad B.*

"I was bound by sin, but I found freedom." *Rob P.*

"I was self-seeking, but I found freedom." *Abi S.*

"I was struggling, but I found freedom." *Mitch S.*

"I was hurt and angry, but I found freedom." *Barbara P.*

"I was fearful, but I found freedom." *David M.*

"I was bound by unforgiveness, but I found freedom." *Nessa G.*

"I was bound with hurt, but I found freedom." *Elli H.*

"I was hopeless and afraid of the unknown, but I found freedom." *Katie B.*

"I was hurt, but I found freedom." *Matthew S.*

"I was addicted, but I found freedom." *Brent W.*

"I was defeated, scared, suicidal, and addicted, but I found freedom." *Leigh Ann R.*

"I was lost and bound, but I found freedom." *Dave D.*

"I was isolated and brokenhearted, but I found freedom." *Chad C.*

"I was full of doubt and fear, but I found freedom." *Victor P.*

"I was bound by sin, but I found freedom." *Christy S.*

"I was living without purpose and unfulfilled, but I found freedom." *Kyle B.*

"I was bound, but I found freedom." *Sophia E.*

"I was tempted by boys, but I found freedom." *Victoria-Kate E.*

Contents

Foreword

Some people are transformed overnight when they surrender their lives to Jesus. They throw their drugs out the window, apologize to the people they've wronged, break off unhealthy relationships, and make a 180-degree turnaround. I love dramatic conversions.

But the process of change is slower for most of us. While the new birth is indeed an instantaneous experience, salvation is not. We aren't just "saved" in an emotional moment at a church altar; we are "being saved" on a daily basis. Like Lazarus, who emerged from his tomb wrapped in grave clothes, we can experience the miracle of salvation and yet remain bound. Jesus told those standing near Lazarus, "Unbind him, and let him go" (John 11:44, NASB). We, too, need someone to unwrap us. And I believe my friend Mark Evans has given us a helpful tool in this new book. The truths in this book will set you free!

I minister to countless Christians who struggle with various forms of brokenness. Some are addicted to behaviors or substances. Others are emotionally crippled because of their upbringing. Still others are haunted by childhood trauma. Often, our advice to them is as insensitive as it is unrealistic. We say, "Get over it. If you're a Christian, you can't struggle with those things."

That's crazy! Christians stumble. While I would love instantaneous change, the Bible speaks of both regeneration (which happens at the moment of conversion) and the "renewing by the Holy Spirit," which is a process (see Titus 3:5). And Mark Evans shows us in this book that the process starts with a changed mind. You must adjust your thinking if you want true spiritual freedom.

Jesus promised He would take us through the steps toward healing. When He began His ministry in Nazareth, He opened the scroll and read:

> "The Spirit of the Lord God is upon Me, because the Lord
> has anointed Me to bring good news to the afflicted; He
> has sent me to bind up the brokenhearted, to proclaim lib-
> erty to captives and freedom to prisoners…to grant those who
> mourn in Zion, giving them a garland instead of ashes."
> (ISAIAH 61:1, 3A)

You may be one of those who mourns in Zion. You may be a Christian, and yet you may be dragging a ball and chain behind you. Something may have a vise grip on your brain, controlling your thoughts and emotions. Many believers who struggle with secret sin or emotional baggage stuff their problems under the proverbial rug and pretend to be free. However, their masquerade usually does not end well.

That's one of the many things I love about Mark Evans: he is real about his own human frailty, and he can even laugh about it. His humor will make you laugh, but it will also disarm you so that you can get honest about your pain. This book might make you laugh and cry at the same time, but the end result will be freedom.

If you are still a captive, please don't hide in the shadows. Identify your brokenness and then recognize that Jesus has provided the grace to overcome anything that binds you. I challenge you to read this book and ask God to change the way you think. God wants to liberate you, but freedom requires brutal honesty and a willingness to talk to someone about your struggle. Today, God is calling His army to assemble. However, we cannot march in step with Him if we are dragging two hundred pounds of chains behind us. It's time to break free.

J. Lee Grady, author
Set My Heart on Fire and other books

Acknowledgments

Thank you to my sweet wife, Robbyn, and my incredible daughters. You each inspire me to be the best human being possible. I enjoy the stories we create and the memories we share. It only gets better with time. Thank you, Olivia, for sharing with me your vision that inspired this book. Thank you, Sophia, for being a devoted reader and making me laugh at life. Thank you, Victoria-Kate, for showing me the kindness of Jesus. Thank you, Stella, for reminding us that we are out of shape. Thank you, Robbyn, for always reminding me to live above and not beneath—to be the head and not the tail, to be a leader and not a follower—and for always encouraging me to pursue the dreams of my heart.

Thank you to my parents for teaching me the ways of God, for living out the pages of the Scriptures in front of me, and for showing me a genuine faith. You modeled Jesus, for sure.

Thank you to my Believers Church family for your prayers, for your giving, and for your patience. I pray the stories in the pages ahead inspire you to live your best life ever—it awaits you.

Thank you to Jennifer Rothwell for the unlimited gift of yourself and your wisdom in helping me write this book. You are a true measure of friendship.

Thank you to Chris Hayes for your incredible design work and using your talents to further God's Kingdom.

Thank you to all my friends for grace, for memories, and for playing a role in the story of my life. May you find joy in the journey that lies in front of you. May you live your passions and pursue your dreams. May you rise above the perils of life and find the beauty that resides in every single day.

And as I always say, "Has anybody told you that they love you today?" I do.

Preface

n spring 1975, a mess was created that was so devastating that it took more than twenty years to clean up. The mess was inside my head and it was ruining my life. One silly thought, dripping like a leaky faucet, created a mess so disastrous that I found myself hopelessly stuck in a cycle of fear and torment. However, on July 31, 1995, at 8:20 p.m., I fixed the leak that had been dripping more than two decades. Now I'm writing to share with you my story. I want to take you on a journey of how I stopped the leak, cleaned up the mess in my head, and found freedom from emotional habits that were robbing my life.

It's my belief that our thoughts can create for us either a mess or a masterpiece. It all boils down to a choice. You can spend your life continually cleaning up a mess or you can get busy enjoying the beauty of a masterpiece. I encourage you to enjoy the beauty of the masterpiece. It makes for a better life, a better home, a better marriage, and a better tomorrow. You no longer have to be trapped in a mess, living beneath your God-given potential. You can find your hope again. Happiness doesn't have to elude you. Your dreams can be realized.

**You never again have to let the mess in your head
ruin the beauty of your tomorrow.**

The Mess in Your Head

"If I've learned one thing in life, it is that emotions sure can make a mess of things."

s there a mess lingering in your head? You're not alone. I've fought my own emotional battles and created my own messes. I've struggled with fear to the point of feeling paralyzed. I've fretted over financial issues to the point of having panic attacks about bills being due. I've allowed my disdain of tense situations to cause me to avoid them at all costs. An issue I hoped to skirt in one area only created a mess in other areas. However, I've finally realized how to stop letting the mess linger around in my own head.

After twenty years in pastoral ministry, I have been privy to more than one occasion to the certain devastation that out-of-control emotions can wreak on any who dare fall prey. I've witnessed the downfall of dozens of men, women, and children thanks to unchecked emotions. My own emotions have made a mess of things. Quite simply, emotions gone awry can produce horrible outcomes in life. I've seen unbridled emotions destroy marriages, annihilate friendships, ruin relationships, and even bring some to a point of such hopeless despair they feel the only way out is suicide.

Your emotions no longer have to create a mess in your head.

Through the years, I've seen just about every mess emotions can make. I've watched jealousy bring a husband to total defeat as he sat with a loaded pistol in hand, asking me to talk him out of murdering his wife's lover. I was there when, following the death of their child, a parent sank into deep, dark depression, leaving them paralyzed and unable to enjoy life. I remember the shock and grief I felt when a friend put a gun in his mouth and took his life while hovering over his girlfriend who was going to leave him. I can't begin to recount the devastation I've witnessed caused by anger, rage, frustration, bitterness, lust, hate, envy, insecurity, anxiety, and fear—all a result of out-of-control emotions.

If I dwell on the emotional carnage I've seen, it's almost disheartening. I've sat through counseling sessions with young girls and boys who have been raped, molested, abused, abandoned, and given up as undesirable and unwanted. I've spent hours trying to convince a bitter wife to forgive her ex-husband. I've had session after session with young men who struggle with their sexual identity because of the emotional trauma they experienced through sexual abuse. To all these people, I've tried along the way to offer help, encouragement, and any godly advice that would bring hope to those in such dire need. These real-life stories are most certainly plentiful. Some ended in a mess. Some ended in a masterpiece. Yet, as much as I long to help people, I have come to realize that the mess going on in a person's head can most certainly sabotage his or her potential of a hopeful future.

Many times, it's the lighthearted emotional struggles
that cause some of the bigger messes.

On a lighter note, there is the more lenient side of our emotional struggles. Minute decisions such as what to eat, what to wear, where to live, whom to marry, and where to go to college are a few examples that can press on our emotions. It would appear that these minor emotional struggles shouldn't carry the weight of those emotions that would leave one suicidal. However, I beg to differ. Many times, it's the lighthearted emotional struggles that cause some of the bigger messes. Something as simple as a nagging weight issue can be so daunting that it leaves one in a whirlwind of hopelessness. To the person in a hurry to get to work, a traffic jam, or even a long red light can be just the trigger needed to set him or her off on an emotional rant. Life, in general, at any time or under any circumstance has the potential to suck anyone into an emotional vortex of misery.

I'm not always certain as to the cause of the leak that begins the drip that eventually makes the mess. Maybe just coming home to a dirty house after a long day at work causes the drip to start. Maybe a husband who is watching TV instead of paying attention to his wife is just the push needed to send her on a downward spiral. Perhaps it's the mouthy child, the nosey in-law, the nagging coworker, or the mean boss who makes you want to pull your hair out in an emotional frenzy. Maybe it's the gossiping friend, or malicious ex-boyfriend who leaves you feeling emotionally nauseated. Perhaps it's the low checkbook balance that screams you're broke. Worse yet, maybe it's the fact that there is no milk left in the refrigerator for your morning cereal and that drives you to insanity. Or the granddaddy of all emotional peril: hearing those dreaded words, "I'm sorry. WE ARE OUT OF COFFEE."

Whether you struggle with tragic circumstances or petty frustrations, one thing is guaranteed: your emotions can most definitely make a mess of things. Your emotional status can make or break you. How you handle your emotions will determine the environment in which you live and the outcome of the life you desire. And I'll let you in on a little secret. If you want a good life, you must learn how to handle those petty, chaotic, nagging, out-of-control emotions before they get the best of you. Your best life awaits you. And no, it's not going to come after you win the lottery. It's not going to arrive after you finally get that new job. Your best life is not even bound to your circumstances—past, present, or future.

Your best life is bound to how well you handle your emotions.

Life happens—good and bad, happy and sad. How you handle your emotions will determine the outcome of your life. Handle your emotions well and a great life awaits you despite your past or present situation. Handle them poorly and it's a guarantee a mess awaits you just around the corner. Don't settle for a mess. Stop tolerating bad emotional habits. Buckle up and get busy about living a fantastic life. Let's get ready to plug the leak and clean up the mess that your emotions have made. It's your choice—a mess or a masterpiece. I say, choose the masterpiece.

Introduction Reality Check

1. Identify a present situation that is causing you some emotional stress.

2. What is your knee-jerk reaction when you are facing an emotional crisis?

3. Identify your most dominant emotion—positive/negative.

4. Can you identify the area your mess may be connected to—money, marriage, work, past unresolved issue?

5. What do you feel is the biggest hindrance to finding your emotional freedom? Is the hindrance tied to a person, a situation, an event?

6. What scares you about your future?

7. How do you see your present emotional state influencing your future?

8. Have you ever used this phrase, "It is what it is"? What was it connected to? Do you believe this can change? How so?

9. How does this apply to your current situation: "Your best life is bound to how well you handle your emotions"?

10. Are you presently tolerating poor emotional habits? Why?

CHAPTER 1
A Little Drip

"Don't let a negative thought turn your life into a mountain of a mess."

The year was 1975. It was the beginning of the drip. The coming devastation would have been easier to recognize had it been an all-out flood. However, a little drip doesn't seem as destructive. A small thought planted in my head started the mess. By the time I realized what was happening, it had become a flood of exhaustion, torment, and fear. The mess was so bad that I was left feeling hopeless. Looking back, I now get discouraged that I allowed something so minuscule to cause me such paralyzing instability. Yet one simple, little drip—a tiny seed of a thought—became planted and started me on a journey of hopelessness. One thought was going to create a mountain of a mess in my life.

You no longer have to be stuck in a cycle of emotional hopelessness.

Hopeless—have you ever been there? There's no more miserable way to live than to find yourself feeling hopeless. It keeps you stuck. It paralyzes you and renders you unable to believe that things could get better. It sucks the joy out of your life. Hopeless—the mind-set that believes change is impossible. Hopeless—a life lived to the drumbeat of "It is what it is"; you expect nothing more and nothing less. Hopeless—you feel you have no option but to give up. Hopeless…

I have discovered through the years that much of the hell we live in today is often due to a mess left over from yesterday. Almost every person I meet stuck in an emotional mess can trace back to a moment in time where an initial thought or event started the leak that caused their mess. I can pinpoint the exact moment the drip started in my own life that catapulted me into my mess. The mess in my head started with one little thought that came from a movie. One vivid image planted in my mind started the drip. And that thought, dripping day by day, turned into a monster of a mess. One simple, little, tiny, no-big-deal thought created a twenty-year mess that almost ruined my life.

I was only ten years old in 1975. That's when it all started. *DRIP! DRIP! DRIP!* I was nestled in the couch of my home in Gadsden, Alabama. I had just settled into watching some TV. Back in the '70s, you actually had to get off the couch and make the effort to change the channel if you didn't like what you were watching. Being too lazy to get up to change the channel, I decided to watch a made-for-TV movie entitled *Death Be Not Proud*, instead of my favorite show, *The Waltons*. However, the outcome of my decision wasn't going to end pretty. It took only one scene in that movie to open up a torrent of bad images and thoughts. *DRIP! DRIP! DRIP!* It may have started small, but it took me from 1975 to 1995 to get a handle on that drip.

Death Be Not Proud is based on the true-life story of a devoted father whose son was diagnosed with a brain tumor. Looking back, I should have opted for watching *The Waltons*. However, I became glued to the television set and watched intently as the story unfolded. I have forgotten the plot since almost forty years have passed, and I have never watched the movie again. Still, I distinctly remember the scene that started the drip. Actor Robby Benson, portraying the real-life story of Johnny Gunther, was standing outdoors, bandages wrapped around his head, having successfully endured surgery for the removal of a brain tumor. The scene had me mesmerized. I couldn't take my eyes off the screen, waiting for the typical movie ending: and they all lived happily ever after. I just knew Johnny Gunther would conquer the brain tumor and live.

To my dismay, however, the movie ended tragically. Johnny died! He DIED. *DRIP! DRIP! DRIP!* I was miserably heartsick. How could Johnny die? *DRIP! DRIP! DRIP!* What happened to "happily ever after"? Every show I watched always ended happily. *The Waltons* always said their good-nights as the lights faded. Tarzan always rescued Jane. Batman always got the bad guy.

The Road Runner always made his great escape at the last minute. Johnny was NOT supposed to die! *DRIP! DRIP! DRIP!* In one moment's time, after seeing Johnny's fate, I became obsessed with one little thought: *What if I die?*

Even to this day I don't like to watch anything that has a miserable, unexpected ending that leaves me feeling heartsick. There's nothing about it I like. And in 1975, this was certainly not the movie outcome I was hoping to see. The unexpected ending kept haunting me. *DRIP! DRIP! DRIP!* It was too late; the image and thought had already been burned into my mind. I kept thinking to myself, *What if I die? DRIP! DRIP! DRIP!*

Most emotional messes start with a single thought.

Have you ever found yourself with a mess in your head? Have you ever had an event or image burned into your mind that you can't seem to shake? You go to bed with it on your mind. You wake up with it on your mind. It shows up in your thought life at the worst of times. No matter how hard you try, the images just keep recurring. Maybe it was a death that brought you loneliness. Maybe it was a divorce that brought you grief. It could have been a fight with a friend that wounded you. Perhaps it is a regretful decision you can't go back and change. Maybe you've been raped, molested, abused, or abandoned, and now you can't shake the images or heal the wounds that these horrible events created. My mess? It all started with **a single thought** that continued to drip over and over. The sad part of it all? It took twenty years before I learned how to conquer that one tiny thought.

Hopeless—it's a downward spiral of crushing fear. For me, it was the one phrase that kept resounding over and over in my mind: *What if I die?* It left me miserable. *What if I die?*—it seemed unshakable. It kept creeping up in my thought life all the time. It didn't matter where I was or what I was doing, I just couldn't get the thought to go away. The constant thought of dying was **suffocating** me. It was like a slow death by suffocation. I didn't feel hopeless overnight. I just lost a little hope every day until I eventually felt overwhelmed and worn out. Be assured, overwhelmed and worn out are two key ingredients of hopelessness. And when you lose a little hope every day, somewhere in your future a mess is awaiting you.

Overwhelmed and worn out are two key
ingredients of hopelessness.

Here's how the mess in your head can get the best of you. Something has to first create a drip. The drip is that unbridled thought that starts you on an emotional roller coaster of negative thinking. If you tolerate a negative thought long enough, a royal mess will be waiting for you around the corner. Over time, the constant dripping of a negative thought will always ruin the beauty of your tomorrow.

Because of my personal inability to shake my negative thought, I became an emotional mess. As I couldn't stop the thought, I did the next best thing. I just tried to ignore the thought of dying. Perhaps if I ignored it, the thought might go away. Yet the fear I so desperately tried to ignore soon became tolerated as normal. I just finally accepted the fear and began thinking, *I'm probably going to die young!* I know it sounds crazy. How could a healthy young man with every reason to be happy be an emotional wreck? It's simple. Rather than conquering the thought, **I ignored it**. But I promise you, ignoring negative patterns of thinking is no way to live life. In fact, it's completely paralyzing. Fact: If you keep trying to ignore negative thoughts rather than conquer them, you're making room for an emotional mess to start brewing.

An emotional mess may not kill you,
but it will certainly suffocate the joy right out of you.

Let me begin by defining what I mean by an emotional mess. An emotional mess is nothing more than out-of-control, regularly tolerated, negative thoughts that linger. If you don't handle negative emotions properly, you will be overcome by chaos. It takes only one little out-of-control thought to leave you in a world of hopelessness. One hint of bitterness, one speck of jealousy, one smidgen of lust can set you on a path to dysfunction. A constant barrage of negative thoughts creates an environment that nurtures damaging and emotionally crippling outcomes. Memorize this equation: *Negative thoughts = a negative environment.*

For me? *What if I die?* was my consistent negative thought. *DRIP! DRIP! DRIP!* I would often lay awake in bed unable to shake the images of death. I went to sleep thinking fearful thoughts. I went to school with it on my mind. It took the joy out of the simple things of childhood. I was stuck in a continual cycle of fearful dysfunction, all because of an ongoing negative pattern of thinking. All of that negative thinking just produced an environment of hopelessness around me. You want to know the sad reality? At ten years old, I was genuinely afraid I would die. As time passed, I just gave in to the horrible lie of believing "It is what it is." One little drip: *What if I die?* One little lie: "It is what it is." They compounded to create a mess in my head that was ruining my life. I was indeed hopelessly paralyzed.

You don't ever have to resign yourself to believing "It is what it is."

Let me encourage you. No matter how bad things seem at this juncture, your situation *can change for the better.* Don't let one little negative thought turn your life into a mountain of a mess. Your life can be better than believing "It is what it is." There's hope for a great future. I stopped my mess. And I want you to know that you can stop your mess. We can do it together. We will locate the leak. We will stop the drip. We will clean up the mess. And we will find the joy of life that's been eluding you. I'll teach you how I found **joy** in the journey. I'll share with you how I found freedom from the drip that made a mess in my head. By the end of this book, I believe you will have a smile on your face and hope in your heart. My faith is that the mess in your head will never again ruin the beauty of your tomorrow.

You can stop the drip that's causing your mess—believe it.

Chapter 1 Reality Check

1. Have you ever found yourself in a situation that left you feeling hopeless? What caused it? Are you willing to do something about it? Are you willing to believe your situation can be different?

2. "One little negative thought"—do you have one? Is there a negative thought that keeps dripping and robs the joy of your day? What is it?

3. Can you identify when the drip started? If so, what event or circumstance is it attached to?

4. Do you have an active plan to combat the negative thoughts or are you tolerating their existence? What is your plan? If you are tolerating negative thoughts, why?

5. How do you feel when you respond in a negatively emotional way? How do you feel in the moment? How do you feel afterward?

6. Is there any area in your life where you have said, "It is what it is"? If so, why have you settled it in your mind to be this way? Why is that line of thinking negative?

7. Make a list of the negative thoughts that are part of your life at this moment in time. Beside each negative thought list the opposite/positive thought you desire to see. Now, determine what needs to happen to get you to move more toward the positive side.

6. How does this phrase influence your present situation: "An emotional mess may not kill you, but it will certainly suck the joy right out of you."

7. "Overwhelmed and worn out"—how does this affect your hope? How does this affect your willingness to move forward?

8. How hopeful are you your situation can change?
   1   2   3   4   5   6   7   8   9   10
   Hopeless   Very Hopeful

9. List at least one way you can begin to help your current situation change.

CHAPTER 2

Hopelessly Paralyzed

"You never again have to believe the lie, 'It is what it is.'"

They sat in my office fifteen feet apart. Even though they were husband and wife, they refused to sit together. What made matters worse was that they refused to look at each other. They had come to me desperate for answers. On the surface, it seemed apparent that they hated each other but somehow this couple had ended up in my office asking for advice. I felt all they wanted me to do was to identify which one was to blame for the hell they were currently experiencing. *He* wanted me to see her controlling ways and acknowledge how terribly she treated *him*. *She* wanted me to see how horrible he was at being a husband. It was a poisonous marriage for sure, and they needed me to point out the spouse most responsible for making it so toxic.

It was a strange predicament. This couple said they were in love but seemingly hated each other. They had become entwined in an endless cycle of anger and frustration and were unable to move forward. They seemed physically healthy on the outside. But inside, they were both perfectly hopeless. Their potential for a good marriage was crippled by their hopelessness. They possessed great potential to be a happy couple. However, their anger and frustration bred hopeless despair. They were experiencing paralysis of potential brought on by the disease of hopelessness.

**Hopelessness is succumbing to the lie that
things will never get better.**

Hopelessness paralyzes you. It paralyzes you to the potential of things getting better. In a hopeless state you can't bring yourself to believe you can move forward. You're left feeling lifeless and stuck. You give up believing anything good will happen and you're left with the thought, *There's no use; it's hopeless.* You resign yourself to an "it is what it is" mentality and lose all hope of it ever getting better. Once you embrace hopelessness and begin to believe "it is what it is," your potential becomes paralyzed. It becomes hard to even imagine life any other way. No matter how people try to encourage you, you feel incapacitated and simply give up. Just like the couple above, you are perfectly healthy on the outside, yet immobilized on the inside. There is no acceptable reason you can't move forward, except that you just can't. Moving forward is impossible because you have lost **hope** of moving forward. The beauty of your tomorrow isn't possible because you're hopeless. Even though people may tell you there's hope, you just can't bring yourself to believe it. And that type of resolve—a negative, not-going-to-make-it mentality—will leave you paralyzed to any hope of getting better.

Never let "it is what it is" become your paralyzing thought.

In the beginning of any crisis, your emotions will always scream louder than your reality. You may get bombarded by thoughts of "You can't," "It won't work," and "It's no use." Time whispers in your ear, "Things won't ever change." However, despite these negative thoughts, you must realize that any mess you are in is not **final**. There *is* great hope! You can rally, clean things up, and walk out of it. It is possible for you to live life to its fullest measure. I can attest to this fact.

It's your willingness to get up and get better that has to be more powerful than giving up. Just because things may seem as if they will never change, you can't throw in the towel. I've have heard it said that "time cures all ills." If this were true, don't you think that we all would be cured by now? With the passing of time, if things don't get better, losing hope becomes an easy alternative. Time moves on and negativity creeps in. It's important not to lose hope because of having to "wait it out." Don't let a week, a month, a year, or even years in a mess force you to give up. Note the following Scriptures:

*"Now faith is the substance of things **hoped***
for, the evidence of things not seen."
HEBREWS 11:1 (NKJV)

"But without faith it is impossible to please Him, for he
who comes to God must believe that He is, and that He
is a rewarder of those who diligently seek Him."
Hebrews 11:6 (NKJV)

Hope is your best friend.

Hope gives you the strength to never give up. Faith is the substance of hope and it's faith that pleases God. So logically, without hope you can't have faith. Therefore, hopelessness can never please God. Why? Because when you are hopeless, you give up before God shows up. Hopelessness will isolate you from God. Hopelessness will make you feel abandoned and alone. God **never** wants you to feel isolated, abandoned, and alone. The truth of Scripture draws you to God, who will be a Father to you and will reward you. Reclaim your hope by settling once and for all that God has not and never will abandon you. God will, in due time, **reward** you. This single thought alone will set hope ablaze in your soul. Don't give up before God shows up.

In spring 1995 (twenty years after my mess began), a ray of hope hit my soul. It was life changing for me, and it shook me out of my hopeless way of thinking. My eyes were opened, and for the first time in a long time, I could see God was working to reward me. My wife, Robbyn, and I were driving along Interstate 181 in Tennessee when she decided to open her mouth and offer me some advice. I understood by the look she was giving me that I was about to hear something I didn't want to hear. I knew it was not going to be pleasant. She spoke and I immediately went into an internal turmoil. Her words ignited the spark that would get hope blazing.

"I don't understand something, Mark. If the devil could kill you, don't you think you would be dead by now?" she quipped matter-of-factly. It ticked me off that she would even ask me such a question. I wanted to return some plausible answer that would silence her lack of compassion for my state of being. However, nothing came out of my mouth even though my insides were reeling. My mind was filled only with a myriad of unanswered questions being posed by me to myself. I wanted to pout and blame her for not understanding. But the more I pondered her question, the more clearly I saw the **answer**.

I started asking myself all the straightforward questions that demanded an answer. *Why wasn't I dead yet? What was I afraid of? How had I slipped this far in my thought life? How had I sunk so low? Why was I hopeless if I truly believed in God?* Twenty years after watching *Death Be Not Proud*, I was asked a question that forced me to acknowledge the one thought that was truly holding me back: *Why have I been afraid of dying for the last twenty years?*

Never be afraid to trust God.

I had no answers. I wanted to refute Robbyn's question with the typical "You don't understand because you have never lived in fear!" But I knew this was a God moment, so I kept silent. God was showing me that my fear had me paralyzed because I had become hopeless. I had **lost** confidence in my faith. I had lost my desire to believe I could be free. I was afraid to trust God. Yet, somehow, I knew God was shaking the foundation of my wrong thinking and bringing me another step closer to His freedom.

Have you ever found yourself in the dark about a situation and then, just as if someone turned on the lights, you saw the answer? You ask yourself, "Why didn't I see this before?" When you finally see the light, it is a glorious moment concerning your freedom. "Seeing the light" is the moment where freedom starts to annihilate failure. *"I don't understand something, Mark. If the devil could kill you, don't you think you would be dead by now?"* The light was on. I was putting the puzzle pieces together in my head. Hope was returning. I had spent years afraid of dying. But I wasn't dead. I was afraid of being afraid. Fear said, "You'll die!" Hope was saying, "You're not dead yet!" Finally, I saw the light.

To win the battle, the potential of hope has to disable the power of hopelessness.

My mind was slowly morphing into a new mode of thinking. It was becoming clear that I could no longer fight from a core of hopelessness if I wanted to be out of my mess. I realized that a fear of dying was a feeling, not a fact. I had feared dying for so long that I was dead to hope. Hopelessness had paralyzed me. But one simple question forced me to see reality. I had been afraid to die, but I wasn't dead. Hope emerged, and I started making some progress. Hope changed me! Hope changed my thinking. Hope changed my desire to give up into a belief I could be better. Hope gave me a reason to fight. Hope got me smiling again. Hope started me believing that God would show up.

If you are feeling hopeless now, your thoughts are attempting to paralyze your potential. I'm here to encourage you that your future of freedom is waiting on you. God has your way out. You don't have to live paralyzed by hopelessness any longer. You may have tried to overcome it for years. Your habits may have held you in bondage, and your dysfunction may be trying to inflict its final blow. But don't fret. I am writing this book to offer you hope and tell you that you **can** and **will overcome** and ultimately realize your best life ever. Don't worry how bleak it may look right now. My thoughts were making a royal mess in my head. But I found the answer. I discovered how to live in a continual flow of freedom. Jesus brought to light the emotions that were creating the mess in my head. Now I want to help you see His light for your future, too.

To make progress, you must ignite hope.

Remember the couple in my office at the beginning of this chapter? They were hopelessly stuck. Their marriage was paralyzed. Well, in a matter of an hour, hopelessness sprouted wings and flew away. I simply asked them one question in hopes the light would turn on. I looked at both of them—fifteen feet apart, refusing to acknowledge each other—and asked a simple question. "If you hate each other so much, then why did you marry?" Their first response was comical. "We should never have married!" they resounded. "So tell me what first attracted you to the stupidity of marrying each other?" I asked again. They both took turns. "It was his smile," she said with a quivering lip. "It was her walk," he confessed. "Her walk?" I asked. "Yeah, the way she walked was so sexy," he said with a sheepish grin. Immediately the emotion of the room changed. Both were now smiling. He got up and moved next to her on the couch. They continued the next fifteen minutes proclaiming why they originally fell in love. Less than an hour later, they were walking out of my office hand in hand, kissing each other, and thanking me for my help.

What happened? Was it magic? Was it my counseling skills? I think not. What happened was that a light was turned on and they saw hope. Hope was ignited. Once hope reentered the room, their situation changed. Once hope was regained, they began to move forward. They found their starting point by finding hope. Rather than out-of-control emotions sparking disaster, **hope** ignited their dreams. **Hope** entered and hopelessness exited. That's how you start making progress: **You ignite hope.**

Hope makes even the worst of things seem possible.

Perhaps your situation is defined by unanswered questions and the bewilderment of any future good. You may feel a deep despair—a death sentence, so to speak. Your mind may be turning flips. Will I ever conquer the fear? Will I ever be at peace? Will I ever live without any guilt of my past? Will I ever overcome all the negative thoughts? Will I ever be hopeful? I believe the answer is a resounding YES! There is hope. Your miracle is on the brink of breaking through. Your tomorrow holds great potential. So don't lose hope and don't let despair get the best of you. Don't let your potential become paralyzed. Hope comes when you **turn the light on**. And when you step toward hope, you'll find freedom.

The Holy Spirit is available to help you identify, crucify, and conquer any negative emotions that may be stealing your hope. Now is the time to stop the cycle and move forward. Now is the time to break free into your destiny governed by God's certain purpose rather than your emotions. No addiction, no habit, no scenario, or any excuse has a right to keep you enslaved to hopelessness. Get up. Shake yourself. Free yourself from the hopelessness that has entangled you. You can do it. I know you can. **Get moving!** I'll ask you now like Robbyn asked me, "If the devil could kill you, don't you think you would be dead by now?" You're not dead. You're very much alive. You're breathing. The fact that you are still alive should turn the light on for you. Why don't you dare to do what you've always been afraid to do?

You don't have to live paralyzed by hopelessness any longer.

Chapter 2 Reality Check

1. Why is it so hard to listen to truth when it hurts?

2. How do you feel when someone confronts you with some advice you don't want to hear? How do you feel when someone challenges your emotions? Explain.

3. Why is this so important: "To make progress you must ignite hope"?

4. Is there an area in your life where you are feeling hopeless? If so, why do you feel such hopelessness?

5. Why does hopelessness seem so paralyzing?

6. Can you define the moment when you lost hope? When was it? What happened?

7. Who can speak into your life and challenge you in areas where you may need to change? Do you have anyone in your life who can say to you, "I love you, but you're wrong?"

8. If a situation can go from hopeful to hopeless, could it be possible that a situation could be reversed from hopeless to hopeful? What would it take for that to happen?

9. Name one thing you can do right now that will bring you hope. Do you need to make a phone call? Do you need to apologize? Do you need to rehearse why you originally fell in love? Do you need to dig up that old dream again? Do you need to write a letter to someone? Do you need to just get away for a day or two and spend some time with God?

10. Why don't you take a moment and write down a list of ten things you are thankful for. Just rehearsing that list over and over will help you regain some hope. If you're feeling hopeless, stop focusing on the negatives and take some time to find the positives.

CHAPTER 3

If You're Breathing, There's Still Hope

"God has kept you alive for such a day as this."

"If you're breathing, there's still hope." It's one of my favorite sayings. I quote it to myself quite often. This statement was my first real step toward freedom. It helped me to regain my hope. I will ask you a question that will spur you on toward hope: "Are you still breathing?" Your answer should be obvious. That's how easy it is to regain hope: if you are breathing, there is hope. Breathe in hope. Breathe out hopelessness. Breathe in hope. Breathe out hopelessness. That's your first step. Just take a breath. If you're breathing, there's still hope.

Reclaiming your hope is the first step out of your mess.

I'm an optimist at heart. I've never been one to throw in the towel and walk away defeated. Yes, there have been times when I have had more excuses than hope. I just refuse to let those excuses make me shrink back and give up. I want you to take note of a few verses tucked neatly away in Scripture. They are surely an inspiration for gaining some hope. A man named Caleb was stuck in an endless cycle of frustration. For forty years, he found himself among a disgruntled group of people wandering aimlessly around the desert. Yet, amid the despair, he finds hope.

10 And now, behold, the Lord has kept me alive, as He said, these forty-five years, ever since the Lord spoke this word to Moses while Israel wandered

*in the wilderness; and now, here I am this day, eighty-five years old. 11
As yet I am as strong this day as on the day that Moses sent me; just as my
strength was then, so now is my strength for war, both for going out and
for coming in. 12 Now therefore, give me this mountain of which the
Lord spoke in that day; for you heard in that day how the Anakim were
there, and that the cities were great and fortified. It may be that the Lord
will be with me, and I shall be able to drive them out as the Lord said.*
JOSHUA 14:10–12 (NKJV)

Don't you love that passage? Caleb has spent forty years going in circles.
Forty years of ups and downs. Forty years of people whining and complaining.
Forty years of the same ol' thing happening day in and day out. Yet, he refuses
to lose hope. I love how Caleb says very matter-of-factly, "God has kept me
alive." In other words, he was stating, "I survived the dysfunction, I made it
through a horrible place. I'm not dead yet, and now I'm ready to come out and
possess all God has planned for me." Isn't that some incredible hope?

God wants you to enjoy life, not merely tolerate it.

Are you, like Caleb, ready to trust God and take the first step out of
your mess? It's up to you. You can keep circling the mountain or you can
stop where you are and rehearse this truth: "I'm still breathing and there's
still hope." The fact is, God has kept you alive for such a time as this. Why?
God wants you to fulfill your life's plan, not merely tolerate your life's circumstances. He wants you to gain hope for your future and not succumb
to your present reality. God has a plan, a purpose, and a destiny waiting for
you. Will you rise? Will you decide? You've been kept alive for such a time as
this. There's no mistake in that—you're still breathing for a reason, and that
reason is hope.

It's why I like the opening sentence of this chapter: "If you're breathing,
there's still hope." Every breath tells me I'm alive. If I'm alive, there's still time.
If there's still time, there's still hope. Learn to hope outside the boundaries of
time. The hope in you becomes greater than the clock ticking down to defeat
you. Never ever let time rob you of hope. You have to get a hold on the same
chutzpah as Caleb and let the promise of God propel you regardless of time
and feelings.

Don't let a long journey in the wilderness
cause you to lose your hope.

When you decide to regain hope, you are deciding to hold on to a promise despite how you feel. You are deciding to live by revelation instead of frustration. Stop for a moment. Reread that sentence again. You can decide to live by revelation instead of frustration. Why live by revelation? Revelation is based on *God's* promises. Frustration is based on *your* problems. Revelation is faith and promise oriented. Frustration is time and problem oriented. Revelation brings hope. Frustration brings despair. Revelation says, "It's possible." Frustration says, "It is what it is." Revelation says, "Get busy living." Frustration says, "Get busy dying."

If you want to stop the mess in your head, you have to start being moved by revelation rather than frustration. You must choose to leave behind the impossibilities of your problems and move toward the possibilities of God's promises. It's time to come out of hiding and isolation and **grab hold** of Divine hope. I assure you it can be done. I walked out of my emotional mess one promise at a time.

You don't have to lie on the floor crying any longer. You don't have to cast off hope and settle for some mediocre emotional life of casual happiness and random relief. My prayer for you is that a new day is about to dawn on your life. God is about to shine His light on your situation and you will find freedom. However, to find freedom you must regain hope. It's impossible to fight when you're hopeless. If you've read this far, you must be willing to press on.

You can walk out of any mess one promise at a time.

One of my favorite movies that inspires me toward the power of hope and perseverance is *The Shawshank Redemption*. It brings me to tears every time I watch it. They are not sad tears. They are inspired tears—tears of hope. Accused of a crime he didn't commit, Andy Dufresne is sentenced to two consecutive life terms in prison. Andy is befriended by Ellis "Red" Redding—an inmate serving a life sentence. After being tormented in solitary confinement, Andy tells Red of his dream of living in a Mexican coastal town. Red feels Andy is being unrealistic but promises Andy that if he is ever released, he will visit a specific hayfield near Buxton, Maine, and retrieve a package Andy buried there. Red worries that Andy's odd request means that he is going to take his own life. But instead, that night, after nineteen years behind bars, Andy escapes. Years later when Red is finally released from prison, he makes good on his promise, and he retrieves the package Andy left for him. In the package, a letter was waiting.

Dear Red,
If you're reading this, you've gotten out. And if you've come this
far, maybe you're willing to come a little farther. You remem-
ber the name of the town, don't you? I could use a good man
to help me get my project on wheels. I'll keep an eye out
for you and the chessboard ready. Remember, Red, hope is a good thing—
maybe the best of things—and no good thing ever dies. I will be hoping
that this letter finds you, and finds you well.
Your friend,
Andy Dufresne

I love that! It's my favorite part of the movie. "Remember, [insert your name], hope is a good thing—maybe the best of things—and no good thing ever dies." It makes me teary eyed. The key to you getting out of your mess is to never lose hope. Hope is the ingredient for going a little further. Hope is the thing that seems unrealistic to everyone else, but it won't let you throw in the towel. Hope tells you something good is on the horizon. Hope says, "The deck may be stacked against me, but I'm not going to fold." Those who regain hope will endure and ultimately overcome. Those who regain hope win the battle. Those who keep hope alive will see their dreams come to pass. Let these words found in 1 Thessalonians 1:3 (NLT) burn into your heart and soul.

"As we pray to our God and Father about you, we think
of your faithful work, your loving deeds, and the endur-
ing hope you have because of our Lord Jesus Christ."

Did you absorb that verse? Endurance is inspired by hope in Jesus. If Jesus is alive, if you are alive, there is hope. So wake up. Shake yourself. Get busy regaining your hope.

When you start with hope, you can end with success.

Let me give you some good news. You are not the only person who's had a mess in his or her head. You're not the only one who has ever felt hopeless. You're not the only one who's been hurt, abandoned, wounded, scared, insecure, angry, bitter, lonely, suicidal, or in hopeless despair. You are not alone. Millions have gone before you. Some failed. Some succeeded. However, I'm writing to tell you that *your life can be a success story.* You can and will come through. You can stay hopeful even in the midst of a crisis. Remember, if you're breathing, there's still hope.

I want you to read Hebrews 11. I would like you to take the next several days and ponder it. Every person in that chapter faced daunting situations, some of them seemingly impossible. Look at this quote about what they endured.

> *Some were jeered at, and their backs were cut open with whips.*
> *Others were chained in prison.*
> *Some died by stoning, some were sawed in half,*
> *and others were killed with the sword.*
> *Some went about wearing skins of sheep and goats,*
> *destitute and oppressed and mistreated.*
> HEBREWS 11:36–37 (NLT)

You've probably never been that deep in a mess, beaten beyond recognition, violently in need of rescue, and desperately beyond hope. Sawn in half? If you knew you were about to be sawn in half for your beliefs, wouldn't that give you a legitimate reason to feel hopeless? It would me.

Incredibly, the eleventh chapter of Hebrews is not one of hopelessness but one of victory. The resounding theme of chapter 11 is one of faith and legendary triumph. It's about faith for life beyond circumstances, faith for life beyond emotion, faith for life beyond the moment, and faith for life beyond the suffering. It's a chapter devoted to one theme, and that theme is meant to inspire you to believe for greatness in spite of any adverse circumstance you are facing. It is written for you to live in the realm of great faith **beyond** anything life brings against you. It is written for your hope. If you are going to regain your hope, you have to start *believing* instead of *whining*. You must learn to believe *in spite of* the circumstances you see.

To regain your hope, you must "believe in spite of."

How is it possible to "**believe in spite of**"? It seems so contrary to human nature to keep hope alive when everything is caving in around you. It's easy to hope when things look hopeful. But you have to learn to keep hope alive on your worst day and against all odds. You have to maintain your hope "in spite of." "In spite of" is why God gives you faith. Faith is given for you to overcome. God never intended for things categorized as "in spite of" to cause you to shrink back. He planned for you to rise above "in spite of" and overcome in all arenas of life. I want you to notice Hebrews 11:1. Before we get started in the process of faith, we are given a glimpse into the essence of faith. Before we read about all the exploits of those who conquered life "in spite of," we notice how they started and how they ultimately achieved their end result.

> Now *faith* is the confidence that what we *hope* for will actually happen,
> it gives us *assurance* about things we cannot see.
> HEBREWS 11:1 (NLT)

Don't you love that verse? I do. It reminds me that the starting line of conquering life "in spite of" is **faith, hope, and assurance**. Your level of **faith** is in direct correlation to your level of **hope**. When hope and faith work together, you can be **assured**. You can once and for all *be certain*. To conquer life you need more than emotions, you need certainty. And faith needs hope if it is to achieve this end.

Where there is hope, there is possibility.

I cannot stress to you enough that it is time to regain your hope. To regain your hope, you must stop allowing the frustrations of your emotional habits to determine the outcome of your tomorrows. To regain your hope, you must focus on the promise and not the problem. To regain your hope, you must live by revelation and not by frustration. To regain your hope, you must realize you've been created and kept alive for such a time as this. To regain your hope, you must stop fretting time. To regain your hope, you must believe your eyes will see what your heart believes. To regain your hope, you simply believe "in spite of." My advice to you is, "Stop the madness." Make a decision **now** to regain your hope that may have dwindled since your battle began. Stir yourself to trust God. Stir yourself to believe He's going to show up. Stir yourself to hope. Take a deep breath…

If you're breathing, there's still hope.

Chapter 3 Reality Check

1. How does "time spent waiting" affect your hope?

2. How does your thinking need to change in order for you to regain your hope?

3. Why is defeat connected to hopelessness?

4. Explain this phrase, "When you start with hope, you can end with success."

5. What does it mean to you to believe "in spite of"?

6. How can this be true: "If you're breathing, there's still hope"?

7. Read Hebrews 11:1. Faith is more than belief—it's being 100 percent certain. Concerning your present situation, how certain are you it will improve?

8. Forget what you may be struggling with at this moment. Discover and list three things that bring you great hope.

9. Explain this phrase: "You must decide to live by revelation instead of frustration." How does this apply to you?

10. Why does it seem so hard to stay hopeful over a long time?

CHAPTER 4

Will God Ever Show Up?

"If God is a Father, then I'm not an orphan."

Have you ever found yourself staring up toward heaven, hands in the air, eyes bloodshot from hours of crying, and wondered, *God, will you ever show up?* It can be disheartening to stand as firmly in faith as you are able, only to feel as if God has abandoned you. No matter how lonely you feel in those moments, you can't let the mess in your head trick you into believing God has forgotten you. Abraham waited twenty-five years for a promised child. Noah took one message from God and worked more than one hundred years building a boat without God ever speaking again. God waited four thousand years to fulfill the promise He made to Eve that her seed would crush Satan's head—but He **did** show up. At just the right time, Jesus entered the world.

Have you ever wondered how different things would be if all the heroes of the Bible gave up before God showed up? Noah would have never finished his boat. He would have given up on saving humanity. No humans, no Jesus. Abraham would not have had Isaac as his son. No Isaac, no Jesus. Mary would not have agreed to be the mother of the Son of God. No baby, no Jesus. And if there were no Jesus, there would be no Savior. No Savior, no eternal life.

These are only four people out of the whole human race, yet their actions—their faith—directed the course of all humanity. You know what's interesting? If any one of these four, at any point in the story, had given up—the course of human history would have been altered. The point?

**You never know what God has planned
down the road, so don't give up!**

One individual who doesn't give up can have a profound impact on the destiny of countless others. Thank God that Noah, Abraham, and Mary did not give up. Eternal life has been made available to the entire world because of such. There's power to be realized when you don't give up. We get a small glimpse into one man's story of never giving up in Luke 2. It's the story of baby Jesus' dedication day and one man's determination to never give up on what God had promised. His name is Simeon. He stood the test of time. He prevailed over the pressures of life, religion, and circumstance. In this story, Mary and Joseph were bringing baby Jesus into the temple, in accordance with Jewish custom, to present him to the Lord and to offer a sacrifice. Hundreds of years had passed since the promise of the coming Messiah was given. Yet Simeon refused to give up on the promise. He spent his life believing in hope. And he knew his eyes would see what his heart believed. Look at what Simeon said:

> *27 Moved by the Spirit, he went into the temple courts. When the parents brought in the child Jesus to do for him what the custom of the Law required, 28 Simeon took him in his arms and praised God, saying: 29 "Sovereign Lord, as you have promised, you may now dismiss your servant in peace. 30 For my eyes have seen your salvation, 31 which you have prepared in the sight of all nations.*
> LUKE 2:29–31 (NIV)

Simeon refused to die until his eyes saw the manifestation of a promise. He refused to even consider defeat. He refused to rely on feelings. He was moved to believe beyond his emotions. He was moved by the Holy Spirit to hold fast to his future. He held on to something greater than his feelings. He held on to a promise. He trusted what God had said, regardless. I love what verse twenty-seven states in the above passage, that Simeon, "Moved by the Spirit went into the temple courts." Simeon was moved by the Spirit to believe that God, the Messiah, would show up. He stayed in the temple day in and day out expecting a Divine intervention. Regardless of time and feelings, he trusted God would show up. Day after day, one belief kept him strong. "God **will** show up and my eyes **will** see Him!" He refused to give up—and God showed up.

To stave off the mess in your head, you must EXPECT GOD TO SHOW UP.

In every crisis you face, you must believe He will show up. If you're apt to believe that trouble is your lot in life, you expect that trouble will always find you. But if you want to see good come of your life, you must expect God to show up. The mess will never leave your head if your expectations are negative and wrong. You have to shift your thinking from expecting the worst situation toward expecting Divine intervention. A shift to the expectation of Divine intervention is where you start thinking and acting like God will show up.

When you shift to expecting Divine intervention, you will begin to see dramatic change in your life. Truth becomes the foundation of your emotional status rather than relying on circumstances and feelings. When you **realign** yourself to Truth rather than aligning with feelings, you release God's help. Grabbing on to a morsel of hope makes it impossible to hold on to the hell on earth your mess has created. Hope and hellish circumstances don't go well together. However, if you surrender hope before God shows up, the outcome will be disastrous. Hopelessness is powerful. It not only affects you, but it can also potentially change the outcome for all those around you. However, the real power lies in believing that the God of the universe will show up for you. It changes how you think about the mess you're facing. Believing God will show up realigns your thinking from negative thinking to **positive thinking**.

Not only do your thoughts have to change—for example, "I choose to destroy negative thinking"—but your expectations also have to change—for example, "I believe my outcome will be good." Your thoughts may be focused on the immediate threat at hand, but your expectations are linked to what lies **ahead**. Hope is about NOW. Expectations are concerned with LATER. Therefore, your expectations will either be hope builders or dream killers. You can't have both. Shifting to a mind-set of Divine intervention will state, "I am what God says I am, regardless of how I feel." Once you begin to expect your outcome to be what God says and not what you feel, your tomorrows can become beautiful. Your expectations become expectations of hope, not misery.

Your expectations should be hope builders, not dream killers.

Once you start expecting God to show up, once your expectations turn toward what God says about your situation, your new thoughts become hope builders. If, rather, you have no expectation for God to do anything concerning your situation, your thoughts remain dream killers. How you handle your expectations is critical. This is why many never find freedom. Their expectation is that God will never show up. They give up before God shows up. A shift of thinking toward Divine intervention says, "It doesn't matter how I feel right now, for I know God will show up, and I shall overcome."

Can you honestly state that your current expectations, regardless of your situation, are for God to intervene and bring about some good? No matter how much hope you have regained, if you don't shift yourself toward **expecting** Divine intervention, you will lose that hope before the help arrives. Many people start out hopeful but lose hope as time passes. When God doesn't answer a prayer on their timetable, they give up. When God doesn't meet their deadline, negativity sets in. Expectation of God ever showing up is lost. And unfortunately, dreams die when hope is lost. If you quit expecting God to show up and help you, then you are abandoned to rely on your own resources and left to clean up your own mess.

Truly, if God doesn't intervene for us, we are the most pitiful people. The great news is that God won't leave you alone, and He doesn't want you to handle life without Him. Believe. Believe that you aren't an orphan left alone to clean up your own mess. Believe. Believe that He's your Father and you are His child. Believe that He **can** and **will** intervene to help you overcome the mess. He will intervene because His Word says He will intervene. Look at the word of encouragement God gives to His people in the book of Deuteronomy in the Old Testament. God's people are coming off a four-decade trek of going in circles. They were given a promise forty years prior but had been sidetracked by fear and excuses. They had settled for their own emotional status, and now God was confronting them about the potential of moving forward:

> *"So be strong and courageous! Do not be afraid and do not*
> *panic before them. For the LORD your God will person-*
> *ally go ahead of you. He will fail you nor abandon you."*
> DEUTERONOMY 31:6 (NLT)

God will never ever abandon you.

Don't you love that piece of advice from God's mouth? I do. They did not have to worry about God abandoning them. They could rest assured He would help. And the result of God never abandoning them and guaranteeing them of His help was strength and courage. It gives me great hope when I feel discouraged and wonder if I really can achieve all God has planned for me. God will personally go before me. He will not fail me or abandon me. I love it! I never have to worry about God leaving me alone to figure out my mess. Let this soak into your mind. Mull on this for a moment: "When you believe God will help you, it gives you strength and courage to keep moving forward." When you believe that God will never abandon you and believe that He will surely help you, strength comes to you. And when you have strength and hope, you can endure until God shows up.

Hear the advice of Jesus given to His disciples. Jesus had been letting His disciples know that a change was on the horizon. They would have to learn to do life from **another mind-set**. Because of the information Jesus shared, they had become slightly nervous about their future. Their hearts had become troubled. However, Jesus spoke with such certainty when He said the following:

> *"I will ask the Father, and He will give you an-*
> *other Helper, to be with you forever,*
> *even the Spirit of truth, whom the world can-*
> *not receive, because it neither sees Him*
> *nor knows Him. You know Him, for He*
> *dwells with you and will be in you.*
> *I will not leave you as orphans; I will come to you."*
> JOHN 14:16–18 (ESV)

You no longer have to live or think like an orphan.

That's great advice. Jesus was promising heavenly help. He was promising help beyond what a worldly mindset could comprehend. He was promising them they never had to worry about being abandoned. That's incredible news. Grab hold of this truth: "You don't have to live with an orphan mentality." Readjust your thinking. Feelings may say, "I've been abandoned." But Truth says, "I have heavenly help from a Father who would never treat me like an orphan." By readjusting your thinking to Truth, you will find courage to keep going.

When I was younger, my mother would tell me, "Mark, you are who the Bible says you are." At first, I just thought that she was quoting some strange religious talk. However, after watching the fruit of my mom's life, I have learned to say, "This is my Bible. I am what it says I am. I can have what it says I can have." I say it over and over. "This is my Bible. I am what it says I am. I can have what it says I can have." I've learned to **readjust** my life to truth of God's Word. I've learned from the Bible that my emotions and feelings do not dictate my outcome. I've learned that God is my Father and I am His child. I've learned that God will always work things out to my good when I live out His purposes. And I've learned that God will always help me. I have a Heavenly Father who **can** and **will** help me. I've finally settled that I never have to succumb to an orphan mentality again.

Grab this truth for yourself: "You don't have to succumb to an orphan mentality ever again." In a moment of crisis and frustration, you can be assured that God will show up. When you align your life with the truth of God's Word, you are aligning with God. When you shift your life to fit what the Bible says about you, God shows up with His favor. He won't abandon you or treat you like an orphan. Holding on to a decision to believe the Bible **regardless** of your feelings will keep you from throwing in the towel every time. Believing what the Bible says about you will keep you believing God will show up regardless of how messy it gets. The great thing about expecting Divine intervention is that it gives you strength to "stay the course" and not jump ship. Can you say this about yourself? "I am who God says I am. I have what God says I can have." It's not just a religious mantra or an emotional exercise.

It's His promise. It's your hope. You can be all that God promises that you can be. And God wants to help you.

When you enlist Divine help, you will find your way out of any mess.

One clear reason many never find real freedom is they jump ship. Feelings and frustrations yank them into the waters to fend for themselves. They get tired of waiting. The feel **abandoned**. They start doubting. Then all the negative thoughts sidetrack their progress. Staying hopeful is hard when you lose sight of the fact that help is coming your way. You can't live one moment as though God is going to help you, and in another moment you're readying yourself to jump ship. Make a choice. Either believe that God will show up to you, or go ahead and jump ship. You can't have it both ways if you want to clean up the mess. I want to encourage you to stay on the ship no matter how rough the waters get. Simply having the **courage** and resolve to stay on the ship is most of the battle. Don't jump ship yet. Hang in there. Have faith that God will show up.

God does not show up because you pout and whine. Pouting says, "If God cared, He would do something about it right now." Faith says, "I trust God regardless." If you pout and refuse to trust Him, you are reacting to your feelings, and you are sliding on a slippery slope that leads to disastrous consequences. You must settle your decision to trust God regardless, expect Him to show up, and not change your mind. Look at what the book of James tells us about wavering back and forth on your decision to trust God:

> *6 But let him ask in faith, with no doubting, for the one who doubts is like a wave of the sea that is driven and tossed by the wind. 7 For that person must not suppose that he will receive anything from the Lord; 8 he is a double-minded man, unstable in all his ways.*
> JAMES 1:6–8 (NLT)

Don't allow some dysfunctional mess to cause you to doubt that God can and will help you.

Double mindedness. It usually goes something like this: "I choose THIS. No, I choose THAT! No, THIS! Wait! THAT. Yes, THAT! Maybe I should stick with THIS?" Constant vacillation and wavering back and forth in your mind-set robs you of Divine help. The child mind-set: "My Heavenly Father will help me." The orphan mind-set: "I might as well help myself." When you make an unwavering decision to trust God, you release the power of God's help. When you bounce back and forth between mind-sets, you are robbed of any Divine intervention. And a life without Divine intervention is a doomed life. Start expecting to see and experience God's help coming your way. Remember, you are not an orphan. You are an **adopted** child of God.

Do you think like an adopted child of God? Or do you think like an orphan? An orphan mentality always sweats the outcome. The adopted child is at rest. An orphan mentality makes one a nervous wreck. The adopted child is at rest. An orphan mentality feels abandoned. The adopted child is at rest. An orphan mentality gives up. Why such a converse difference? Because the orphaned child is consumed with fixing his or her own mess while the adopted child assumes a posture of rest. The adopted child knows that God will show up. He or she is at rest. Not sweating the outcome. Not being a nervous wreck. Not feeling abandoned. The adopted child assumes a position of victory before the victory ever comes. How? The adopted child stays fixated on the promise and not the problem.

**You will find great peace when you realize
God has adopted you despite your mess.**

Years ago, something happened that taught me about the posture of being at rest. I was tired of trying to "find my answer." I had been struggling for weeks with fear and this particular morning was no different. I was getting ready for my day. I was in the shower crying in self-pity, feeling completely defeated, when I heard a voice say in my heart, "JUST BELIEVE!" Immediately, I felt refreshed. "JUST BELIEVE!" My mind raced. *How could I have forgotten to believe?* I thought. *Am I not believing?* I had been praying, crying, asking, quoting Scripture, and doing anything else spiritual I could find to do. I began frantically examining myself. *Had I not been believing this entire time?*

I jumped out of the shower as fast as my soapy feet would carry me. I grabbed my Bible and began searching the Scriptures until I found a verse about believing God. The verse is found in the book of Hebrews and gives clear insight to what happens when you really believe.

"For we who have believed enter that rest…"
HEBREWS 4:3 (NLT)

When I found that verse, I understood just what God was speaking to my heart. He could see far beyond my Scripture quoting, miles past my tears, and deeper than my religious behaviors could sustain me. He saw my heart. Even though my head was believing, I was still a nervous wreck. Why? I wasn't at rest. I had all the right Scriptures in my head, but I wasn't even close to being at rest. I was quoting Scripture like a pro, but was failing miserably at trusting God. God knew the condition of my heart, and He was exposing it.

The fruit of my heart wasn't at rest. I was in torment. Sure, I was quoting God's Word, but I never found rest in what I was quoting. I was frustrated, exhausted, pouting, fighting, and praying but doing nothing remotely resembling resting. When I would sense the fear coming, I would begin to experience feelings of dread. I would quickly quote a Scripture and immediately begin to pray frantically. Even so, I can attest that I never felt any emotion connected to rest. I knew then that the only way rest was going to come was by my believing that God would show up without my giving up.

Expecting God to show up before you give up is a necessity if you want to overcome the mess in your head. Why? It puts you in a posture of rest. When you're expecting God to intervene, you don't worry about your situation. You're at rest. Rest is a hope builder. See how this works? You start expecting God to show up. Expectation of God's help builds your hope. Your faith says He WILL show up. And when you trust God will show up, you are at rest. No more emotional mess. Heavenly rest is a good thing—a necessary thing. That's a good point to ponder. Has your mess met His rest? When you decide to trust God *regardless*—when you believe what the Bible says about your situation *regardless*, when you determine to never jump ship *regardless*—you can be at rest because you have settled once and for all that GOD WILL SHOW UP.

Your emotional mess can be transformed by God's heavenly rest.

Chapter 4 Reality Check

1. Why is it so tempting to GIVE UP before God SHOWS UP?

2. How would you define God's favor toward you?

3. Do you struggle believing God will show up to help you? Explain.

4. What would need to change for you to state, "God showed up."

5. Has your earthly mess met His heavenly rest? How do you know? Are you at rest or are you still struggling emotionally?

6. How is expecting Divine intervention a hope builder?

7. How is REST the sign of your believing? What emotions pull on you to not be at rest?

8. What is your emotional result when you spend your energy sweating the outcome? Is this emotional result worth your energy?

9. How is it possible to master some religious behavior, such as quoting Scripture, but fail miserably at trusting God?

10. How will you display a "child mentality" rather than an "orphan mentality" concerning your situation?

CHAPTER 5

There's a Miracle in Your Mess

"Bad news may knock you down, but it doesn't have to knock you out."

Have you ever jumped out of bed, ready to face the day, with things going along as planned, when suddenly your day gets turned upside down? Your dreams become shattered in a moment's notice. You wake up and never expect to face what's in front of you. As quickly as breath is leaving your body, your life turns into a nightmare. It's the kind of day where bad news comes without invitation.

Unexpected and unwanted is typically how bad news comes calling. It rarely comes with invitation. Bad news just shows up unannounced and un-welcomed. Nobody likes to hear it. On those days, how nice it would be to just climb back in bed and get a do-over. How wonderful if we had the ability to just restart the day and never hear the crushing news that brought a mess to the day. I've never met a soul who revels in bad news. No one longs for days full of hell, pain, and sorrow. And fittingly so, on the heels of bad news is where emotional mess finds its strongest hold.

It's no surprise that bad news is negative thinking's best friend.

I don't know how your bad news arrived, but I'm almost certain that somewhere in your journey, bad news came knocking on a day you least expected. Maybe it was when your spouse was leaving after twenty-six years of marriage. Maybe it was the phone call that said your child had been in a horrible accident. Maybe it was the day you miscarried your baby. Maybe it was when your boyfriend broke up with you. Maybe it was the notice that came in the mail stating you were soon to lose your house. Maybe it was the first time you embraced suicide as a good option. Maybe it was when you discovered throwing up could control your weight-gain fears. Maybe it was the first time you became drawn into the powerful addiction of prescription drugs. Maybe it was the dreaded words, "You have cancer." Maybe it was when you were molested. I don't know when bad news first knocked on your door, but I'm sure it's clear to you.

Don't let bad news start you on an emotionally downward spiral.

On Friday, May 19, 1989, bad news called me personally. It was the day death came knocking on my door. I was enjoying a typical day in the office, working on designing a T-shirt for our upcoming youth summer camp. Our secretary, Mary, buzzed me in my office, stating that I had an urgent call on hold. I took the call, never knowing how bad news was about to change my life.

Mr. Evans?
Yes.
Are you the husband of Monica Rowland Evans of Statesboro, Georgia?
Yes, this is he.
I am calling to let you know that your wife has been in a car accident.
Accident?
Yes.
Is she OK?
You need to hurry and get to the hospital in Burke County.
But is she OK?
You need to hurry and get here to the hospital.
But I need to know if my wife is OK!
I can't give you that information over the phone.
Well, you need to tell me if she's OK or not!
Mr. Evans, you need to get here as soon as possible...

I immediately hung up the phone, and Mary and I began the forty-five-minute drive to the hospital. I felt like my head was going to explode. Every dreaded thought felt like a jackhammer in my mind. *"What IF?" "How could God let this happen?" "What happened?" "Is she dead?" "Death?" "Is Monica dead?"* I felt like I was the victim in some horror movie. As we sped down the road, I couldn't help but imagine horrendous possibilities. Worst-case scenarios flooded my thoughts. Worst-case scenarios—they are the nuclear fuel for igniting a cataclysmic mess in your head.

Never let bad news define you.

When I arrived at the hospital, I hurried to find the nurses' station. Intercepted by several nurses, I was whisked away to a cold and dreary side room. A few moments later, two more nurses and a physician were standing beside me. Five strangers were standing silently in a tiny gray room. It was nothing like Hollywood depicts. An eerie feeling came over me. Everyone in the room possessed a noticeably sad demeanor. Even though the room was full of medical personnel, I felt alone, isolated, scared, and sick. One of the nurses had tears in her eyes, and the rest of the staff were obviously shaken. At that moment, I realized death had finally found me.

"Mr. Evans?"
"Yes!"
"I'm sorry, but your wife didn't make it. We did all we could. We bagged her at the scene but were unable to resuscitate her. I'm so sorry. We tried our very best."
"It's OK. I know you did. But she can still live!"
"No! Mr. Evans, she is dead. I'm sorry that this is the case."
"She will come back! She will live!"
"Mr. Evans, we tried all we could. Your wife is gone. She is deceased. She won't be coming back."
"Well, one person died and came back and that is all that mattered. JESUS died and came back, so I know she can come back."
"Yes, He did. But..."
"Well, that was enough for all of us. If Jesus came back, then that is good enough."
"That may be so, but your wife is not coming back today."
"Maybe she won't come back today, but one day she will!"

With my last statement the room fell deathly silent. My mind was in a chaotic whirlwind looking for reasons and answers. I had no script to follow. I felt the room spinning as I searched for something to say or do. Everyone in the room remained silent, tears filling their eyes. Suddenly, all were attempting to console me. One nurse finally came over and put her arm around me. She gave me a hug and stated it would be OK. I asked if we could join hands and pray. They all obliged my request, and I began to pray for each of them individually and laid hands on them all. I asked for peace, hope, life, and resurrection. At the end of my prayer, something transpired beyond my own human understanding. Despite the torrent of bad news, powerful peace came into that moment of despair. It truly was incredible.

One by one, those hospital staff slowly made their way out of the room, leaving me with only one of the nurses. She walked me down the hall, and we waited by the room where Monica was placed. The coroner opened the door and took me over to a gurney covered in a white sheet. Under that sheet with several small bloodstains on it lay my worst-case scenario. It was Monica. My wife. How sad I was. Life was so unfair! Death was no longer just a negative thought of mine. Death was real. The thing I had always feared, the **one little thought** I always pondered, had finally come to pass.

My eyes welled up with tears as I gazed over Monica's lifeless body. I asked the coroner for a moment alone, and he slipped quietly out the door. Monica and I were alone. The whole day seemed to be playing a chorus line of bad news. I began to feel the weight of regrets. *DRIP! DRIP!* How I wished to have said a better good-bye to Monica that morning. If only I could go back in time and say one final, "I love you." Guilt, anger, and frustration riddled my thoughts—*Why me? Where did I go wrong? How could God let this happen?*

Don't let bad news cause you to feel isolated and abandoned.

The bewilderment I felt was crushing. The sense of isolation I experienced was excruciating. I didn't know what to do. Talk about feeling like an orphan. I had no way to phone anyone. No friends were in proximity to comfort me. I was used to tolerating death in my mind, but I was not prepared to tolerate the death on the table in front of me. I was destitute of any plan or step-by-step guide to aid me in dealing with the oppression of unexpected death. *Where was God when Monica needed Him most? DRIP! DRIP! DRIP!* I could feel resentment rising in my heart concerning God and His ability to keep me. The mess in my head was shouting, *"God abandoned me!" DRIP! DRIP! DRIP!*

In that moment of crisis and feeling abandoned, I did what I had always been taught to do. I leaned over Monica's body and laid my hands on her head. I prayed this simple prayer. *Heavenly Father, I know you can raise the dead. I have no doubts in my mind. You did it once; you can do it again! I speak life to Monica and command her to come back.* I kept my eyes tightly closed expecting the power of God to enter the room. I wanted His presence to fill the atmosphere and breathe His life into Monica's body. I waited in expectation. The room was still. The air was calm. But nothing happened despite my passion for God to prove His power.

I felt like this moment could have been God's chance to increase His fame. All He needed to do was raise Monica from the dead and BOOM, citywide revival would break out. This was God's big chance to prove His power to humanity. I guess, however, that God wasn't trying to prove anything because nothing happened. ZERO. A big goose egg was the only answer I got. No life emerged. No wife sat up. No miracle manifested. Nothing was any different after my prayer than before my prayer.

I was shocked and upset that God had not come to redeem His own character. Despite what I thought God should do, God did not do anything. **NOTHING!** Obviously, He was not going to answer my prayer. Death was certain and God was silent. Hope was gone. I felt defeated. It bothered me that I seemed to lack the power and ability to accomplish a miracle. It bothered me that God didn't seem to care to do anything about it to make my situation better. *DRIP! DRIP! DRIP!*

I was sick to my stomach. My entire body ached with sorrow. I was angry. I was frustrated. I felt lost, empty, torn, and confused. I wanted to blame God for His oversight in protecting one of His kids. *DRIP! DRIP! DRIP!* I felt like running away. What was God doing to me? What was He asking of me? I got no answers. So I closed my eyes and raised my hands and, strange as it may sound, I started to sing.

I worship You, Almighty God
There is none like You.
I worship You, O Prince of Peace
That is all I want to do.
I give You praise for You are my righteousness.
I worship, Almighty God
There is none like You!

This story would seem miraculous if I could state to you now that Monica came back to life after that tune. However, that is not what happened. What did occur, however, gave me insight into finding freedom. Freedom doesn't always come in the expected way. Freedom isn't always connected to a single prayer. Freedom may not always come in the moment, but it **always** comes via the process. Know that when you feel the crushing blow of misery in the moment, that's not a sign God has abandoned you. An unanswered prayer doesn't mean He doesn't care. A hellish moment doesn't mean He will never show up. Often, it simply means you have to learn to **trust** God past the moment and through the process. And when you are facing your biggest mess ever, believe me, somewhere in the mess a miracle is brewing.

Freedom is not a MOMENT. Freedom is a PROCESS.

I didn't get a miracle in the moment. What I did get was an understanding of trusting God in the process. The miracle I got wasn't an instantaneous resurrection. The miracle I got was learning to trust God. I learned to trust God when I had no evidence He was there or even cared. I learned to trust Him *past the mess.* I learned to trust Him *all the way through the process.* I received my miracle. The miracle was to trust Him with zero evidence. Even though my situation didn't change, I miraculously felt resolve and peace because I knew that I could trust God all the way through the process.

You can always trust God to make a miracle out of your mess.

I cannot clearly express in words what happened in that room that day, but I do know God started me on a journey of turning my mess into a miracle. A miraculous resurrection did not occur, but a miraculous intervention did. God met with me at my worst juncture of life and asked if I could trust Him. In that cold room, in that hellish moment, I kissed Monica good-bye, covered her face with the sheet, and turned to go. Grabbing the doorknob, tears flooding my eyes, my mind raced, and I heard the following:

"Mark!"
I was startled.
"Mark!"
The voice resounded again. I knew this was God's voice intervening into my world.
"Yes?" I replied.
"Do you think Monica would rather live with you in Statesboro or live in heaven with Me?"
That question seemed so unfair, but I answered, "Anyone would choose to live in heaven with You."
"Do you think Monica would rather be married to you or married to Me?"
This question seemed to cut to the quick. Again, it didn't seem to be a fair question. How could I be expected to answer? Hard as it was, I answered, "She would choose You! Anyone would choose You!" God said to my heart, "Then the case is settled. She is with Me."

Facing fear was hard enough. But burying my wife? It was unimaginable. A funeral for a wife barely past twenty years old—nothing in life was supposed to turn out this way. The tormenting thoughts that came to me with her death were unbearable. *DRIP! DRIP! DRIP!* Always on the heels of my peace was the frustration of my fear. I was attempting to hold myself together on the outside while in actuality, I was falling apart internally. I had to keep forcing myself to believe that a miracle could come out of this mess if I just wouldn't give up.

I did my absolute best in the years that followed Monica's death to stay true to God's peace and not give in to fear. Sometimes I would be fixated on the fear. At other points along the way, I would be 100 percent confident God would show up. I would struggle so hard to ignore the fear. However, despite trying, crying, whining, and praying, I was unable to make much headway at finding freedom. It didn't really seem to me that God was making a miracle out of my mess. I was constantly looking for the miracle in the moment, yet all the while, God was working a miracle through the process.

I want to assure you of something. Despite the mess that was in my head, I am living proof that a person can make it out of a mess. It may seem as if you're living in your worst nightmare. Don't give up. You will get **better**. You can go from a bad place to a great place if you will just step out to trust God in the process. Don't hang your head in defeat. Get a vision for your future and start making headway. There will be a **day** where you look back and see that God's glorious mercy was working all the time. There will come a day where the mess at hand will merge with God's miracle power. The mess will be trumped by good news. The mess will succumb to the miracle. Freedom will find you and the process will be complete.

**Your freedom may not always be in the moment,
but it will always be in the process.**

I'll never forget the day the miracle met my mess. On July 31, 1995, 8:20 p.m., at 120 Cornerstone Drive in Johnson City, Tennessee, I found the freedom that had eluded me for twenty years. Finally, God's miracle bumped into my mess. Hopelessness left in a moment's notice. I could see light at the end of the tunnel for the first time in a long time. On that day in July, I broke free from fear's torment. I drew a line in the sand, and twenty years of an emotional mess came to a screeching halt.

I want to share with you what I have come to realize about breaking free from the cycle of emotional dysfunction and putting an end to emotional messes. I want to teach you how I overcame the mess in my head and found a life of glorious happiness. I want to teach you how to end the drip. That's why I've written this book. I've written it because I found freedom. I put it down on paper because I've met others who are free. I penned my story because I talk to people all the time who are seeking to find freedom. I'm writing to

you because **your** freedom makes it a worthy cause. This book is to teach you about the PROCESS of freedom so you can, once and for all, live free.

If you give God time, He can sculpt a masterpiece from the ashes of your mess.

Now nearly forty years after that first thought of dying, I see clearly and distinctly how to break the spell of the aggravating negative thought patterns that come to shipwreck our lives. Almost thirty years after Monica's death, the process is complete, and I have been radically restored in every realm. I have a wonderful marriage, four great daughters, and I'm no longer an emotional mess. I am confidently positive that despite the mess bombarding your present reality, you can find freedom. And I am 100 percent certain that God can bring a miracle out of any mess. Do you believe that? Out of ANY MESS—a miracle. He's done it countless times before, and He can certainly do it again.

I am living **proof** that God can bring a miracle from the ashes of a mess. It felt like fear was winning out. When fear kept resurfacing, I felt hopeless. When prayers went unanswered, I wondered if God even cared. When death came knocking, I felt terrified. In the moment, I felt defeated. In the moment, my thoughts were total chaos. In the moment, I wrestled with my own faith and ability to overcome. Then, I finally learned that freedom is more than a moment. It is a **process**.

God brought me a miracle from what seemed my worst mess. Jesus has fully and completely restored every lost hope and broken dream and continues this day to amaze me at how His grace is truly sufficient. So let me encourage you. **Hang in there!** Your present moment may look like a royal mess, but I assure you God will bring about a royal miracle. He has the ability and power to make something good out of anything bad. Don't focus on the moment. **Focus** on the process. The moment may say, "MESS," but the process says, "MIRACLE." **Live** the process. **Expect** the miracle.

Regardless of how you feel, there is a miracle residing behind your mess.

Chapter 5 Reality Check

1. Have you ever found yourself facing a crisis of bad news? How did you handle it?

2. When you hear bad news, what is your initial emotional response—anger, frustration, guilt, fear, depression?

3. What hinders you most in believing your mess can turn out good?

4. How does this apply to you: "If you give God time, He can sculpt a masterpiece from the ashes of your mess"?

5. Have you ever felt that God abandoned you? If so, how and in what way?

6. Have you ever found yourself unable to control erratic thoughts? What are the end results of those thoughts? How does it leave you feeling?

7. "Your miracle may not be in the moment but in the process." Are you more focused on the MOMENT or the PROCESS?

   *When you are MOMENT focused, you will stay frustrated more readily. You have to learn how to become PROCESS focused. PROCESS focused means you realize that everything doesn't have to change today. You simply make small steps forward on a daily, weekly, and monthly basis.

8. What is a small step you can take today to help you get through the moment? What one small thing—a thought, an action—can you change today to begin the process of moving toward freedom?

9. What is it that hinders you from staying steady through the process?

10. Write down some statements of your believing that focus on the miracle rather than the mess. I call these miracle statements. Miracle statements are sentences you rehearse over and over, stating what you believe to be possible. They cause you to speak to the potential and not to the problem.

CHAPTER 6

Conquering Your Chaos

"Things were going so well, then I woke up."

'm often asked, "What made you want to write a book about the mess of emotions?" I usually quip back my response, "Because I live in a house with five women!" It's true. After years of living with a wife and four daughters, I have discovered that emotions often influence the level of chaos in your life. About the only time emotions go on break is while you're asleep. So, if you want to live your best life ever, you will have to face up to and conquer the emotions that are wreaking havoc on your life. When you do, you will be well on your way to ending the mess and conquering the chaos.

If you don't govern your emotions,
you are guaranteed a mess 100 percent of the time.

I've had to rethink a lot of my own emotions living in an all-girl environment. I've had to rearrange most of my "manly" emotions just to survive. I cry at chick flicks now. I take long baths at night and ponder what I'll wear in the morning. I watch the *Bachelorette* and other "girly" programs so I can participate in conversations around the house and appear savvy when it comes to feminine topics. Secretly, I watch the Lifetime movies my daughters have recorded and find myself enjoying their crazy plots. All the fellows are feeling sorry for me. I've traded blood, guts, and action for glam, glitz, and drama. Because of all the estrogen floating around the house, I often find myself thinking, *I can't do a thing with my hair! Short? Long? Bangs? I have nothing to wear! I have a pimple. My shoes don't match my outfit!* Ugghhhhh!

I feel as though I qualify as quite an expert when it comes to understanding female emotions. I would like to enlighten you on a few of my discoveries about emotions living in a home with all girls. These pearls of wisdom have been acquired through years of observation. For example, did you know that a common cockroach can make a room full of women begin to disrobe? Yes, it's a proven fact. At least it's the trait of all the girls in my house. They see a roach and they start throwing shoes, flip-flops, shirts, belts, and even hair bows to rid our environment of the poor creature. And that's just the beginning of the emotional bug-killing chaos.

If my daughters see a spider, it's like the apocalypse. Magazines and pillows are taken up as ammunition against the spider. Blood-curdling screams penetrate the house. They all run from the spider and huddle up in mass. When I heard the screams resounding through the house, I assumed that our dog must have been hit by a car. I came running down the stairs full stride. The girls were screaming, shivering, and shaking. "What's wrong?" I hollered. They shouted back, "A SPIDER!"

My heart almost stopped. I thought to myself that a brown recluse or a dreaded black widow must be lurking behind our couch. I formulated my strategy and prepped myself for some brutal spider killing. I asked for the location of the eight-legged monster. They all pointed in unison to the wall. "THERE!" "Where?" "THERE!" "Where?" We kept going back and forth about the precise location of the spider. I made my way slowly toward the wall, shoe in hand ready to perform my heroic, fatherly duty. And there, on the wall, was the horrific creature…so tiny I could barely see it. "KILL IT! KILL IT, DADDY!" I took my thumb and mashed away the tiny intruder.

Out-of-control emotions create an environment of chaos.

At that moment I realized the true level of chaos that emotions can cause. After performing my lifesaving tactics of spider smashing, my wife, Robbyn, said to me, "You mashed him on my wall! Now my wall has spider guts all over it! Why did you mash him on the wall?" Now, as a man I'm thinking a simple thank-you would have been nice. Or perhaps even a "Yay, Daddy saved the day!" But nope, I got none of that. In less than eight seconds, the room went from the screaming torments brought on by a common house spider to frustrations brought on by the incorrect method for spider extermination. I was then informed that the only acceptable way to kill a spider is with hair spray. The manliness in me won out, and I mashed spider guts on the wall instead of using hair spray. Had I only known. What I thought was a heroic exploit, in truth, only produced another frustration. And that was my discovery. If you don't know how to govern your emotions, frustration ensues, regardless of effort.

Out-of-control emotions lead to frustration, and they can also paralyze you from making any progress. For example, even though I struggled with fear of dying as a kid, I never gave a second thought to dying someday by frog bite. But my children have enlightened me to the horrors of frogs in our pool. You see, hiding behind that little white trap door leading to the skimmer basket of our pool was a small green frog. I shall call him Herman. Herman looked a little weathered and rather scared. He weighed in all of about four ounces. Yet not one of my daughters would clean out the skimmer basket thanks to good ol' Herman. My wife would not dare venture her hand into that "gross, slimy, nasty, critter-ridden" basket. Literally, not one member of my family wanted to clean the skimmer basket for fear that Herman might suddenly jump out and attack them, pee on them, give them warts, suck their eyes out, or dare drag them down into the skimmer and feed them to a million baby frogs waiting to feast on the delicacy of human flesh. The truth is, their fear of a small green frog paralyzed their ability to perform the simple task of cleaning the skimmer basket.

I know you are probably thinking, *Just MAKE them clean the skimmer basket!* Yet here's my dilemma. To you and to me, it's just a pool skimmer basket containing a harmless frog. To my girls, however, it's a horror movie. It's not even about their unwillingness to do it. It's more about their **fear** of doing it. Silly as frog fear may seem, it's still fear. Fear paralyzes them from reaching their hand into the pool skimmer basket. Fear of the unknown, fear of something "otherly" grips their emotions so tightly that they are paralyzed and unable to perform the simple task. They have said to me time and time again, "Please, Daddy, don't make us clean the pool skimmer." Perhaps it is rather comical that they can't bring themselves to do it, but it marks a certain truth:

Out-of-control emotions hinder progress.

My family's false belief of Herman's ability to inflict harm is slightly more revealing. The horror does not lie in the chilling possibility of a small green frog devouring the hand of a teenage girl. The horror is in the perception that a pool frog is deadly. Did you catch that? To you and me, it's just a pool frog. To my girls, the threat is imminent. To them, it's a DEADLY pool frog. The horror is in the perception. Their perceptions govern their reality.

My frustrations with roaches, spiders, and pool frogs pose a fact relevant to us all. *Thoughts influence reality.* Roaches, spiders, or frogs—it all starts with how you think about them. Here's a simple truth: *Your thought life governs the environment that surrounds you.* If your thought life is negative, your environment will be negative. Again, it's your thought life that can have the greatest influence over the environment that surrounds you. It's why it's easy to make fun of someone who's afraid of a pool frog. Your perception says, "Harmless!" Their perception says, "Deadly!" Herman is harmless. That's true. Herman is deadly. That's true. Both statements are true, not based on facts but based on **perception**. How Herman is perceived determines whether or not he's a cute frog or a deadly frog. Perception determines reality and that reality can be a hard pill to swallow.

Your emotions determine your environment.

Grab hold of this truth: *Your emotions determine your environment.* It's why we often hear, "If Momma ain't happy, ain't nobody happy." If Momma's emotions go unchecked, everyone in the vicinity will suffer the hellish outcome. When negative emotions are left unbridled, your quality of life will drastically decline. Control your emotions and you can control your environment. Out-of-control emotions lead to a life that is surrounded by chaos. Controlled emotions lead to a life that is settled and at peace. So, to conquer the chaos in your life, you first need to conquer your emotions.

Behind every mess is a negative thought.

Most who come to me for counseling struggle more with negative thinking and perceptions than anything else. To clean up the mess, we have to clean up the thought life. To conquer the chaos, you must first have the right perceptions. The leak has to be prevented before the drip ever starts. Even though God desires to give you a wonderful life, if you fail to handle your emotions correctly, it's a guarantee that your dreams will be thwarted.

Did you know that the emotions given to you by God to help you function and enjoy life can become the very masked marauders that rob you of your best life? When your emotions roam outside the will of God, you will fall prey to chaos. If you want to live free and see your dreams realized, you must handle your God-given emotions in a God-pleasing manner. If emotions rule you, **chaos** rules you. If you rule your emotions, **peace** rules you.

To conquer the chaos, you must recognize that emotions can trick you and deceive you. This emotional trickery is why someone may think, *Nobody likes me!* when, in fact, he or she has plenty of friends. It's why the skinniest person in the room struggles with feeling fat. It's why the healthy person obsesses over the potential of being sick. It's why the insecure person feels that no one likes him or her. People's emotions have skewed their perceptions. They've been **tricked** into thinking one way, when in reality, the true perception is the complete opposite. They've been misguided by emotion. However, when you learn to govern your thoughts properly, you don't end up riddled by a life of frustration and failure.

**A better life is guaranteed when you stop
tolerating negative thoughts and perceptions.**

Remember, negative thoughts create a negative environment. I can assure you that the very emotional struggle you are facing doesn't have to keep you in a continual cycle of frustration. You can break free. You can conquer the hell that emotions are causing. You can win over the frustrations and failures you are experiencing. It is fixable. When you come to an understanding of how to rule your emotions, whether in circumstances, relationships, friendships, events, or in decision-making, you can conquer the chaos.

Did you get that? You **CAN** conquer the chaos. You don't have to live as a prisoner to your own chaos. You can overcome and finally be free. You don't have to live in a continual negative environment of misery. You don't have to stay irritated, aggravated, fearful, anxious, angry, or hurt any longer. You don't have to bow down to the failures of yesterday or the fears of tomorrow. Negative perceptions no longer have to dictate your reality. Negative thinking doesn't have to dominate you any longer. There is a way out. You can live in an ongoing environment of peace, rest, and great success.

Your chaos can be conquered.

How? The beginning point of breaking free is to believe that the chaos can be conquered. The worst place for you to be mentally is thinking that your mess is going to win out, that you will never see a miracle. It may look bleak at this present moment, but I want to stir you to believe. I want to increase your faith so that your feelings *bow* to your faith. Your faith needs a foothold. The foothold of your faith begins with what the Bible says:

> *Jesus looked at them and said, "With man it is impossible, but not with God. For all things are possible with God."*
> MARK 10:27 (NLT)

Let that sink in a minute. It's a simple thought. With God, all things are possible. Remember how one little thought can create a mess or inspire a miracle? Rather than succumbing to the mess that's staring you in the face, dare to believe a miracle can arise. It may feel like it's impossible with you but not with God. Negativity may be surrounding you on all sides right now. It may look impossible. BUT NOT WITH GOD. It bears repeating: *For all things are possible with God.*

Your marriage may be in a disastrous mess BUT NOT WITH GOD. Your fears may keep you up at night and you can't seem to shake the torment BUT NOT WITH GOD. You may feel tired, anxious, worried, broke, mad, frustrated, and hopeless BUT NOT WITH GOD. All of your thoughts may be screaming fear and failure BUT NOT WITH GOD. You have to let this sink deep down into your heart. When God is in the mix, there's always possibility. Take a moment and rehearse it now. Ponder your mess, then speak to that mess, and tell it, *ALL THINGS ARE POSSIBLE WITH GOD.* When you settle this truth, you will be well on your way to conquering the chaos.

**All things are possible with God and that
includes conquering your chaos.**

Chapter 6 Reality Check

1. What are some "perceptions" that try to govern your reality in your life and home?

2. Why are perceptions so critical to reality?

3. Have you seen this at work in your life: "Out-of-control emotions create an environment of chaos." How has it impacted you?

4. Explain how a negative thought impacts your environment.

5. Identify the specific negative thought that's creating the chaos.

6. If "all things are possible with God," why would you ever need to worry?

7. Why is this true: "Out-of-control emotions hinder forward progress"?

8. Describe what this means to you: "When your emotions roam outside the will of God, you fall prey to chaos."

9. Why would the beginning point of hope be "all things are possible with God"?

10. Your emotions affect the chaos in your life. Your emotions affect the peace in your life. Which side do you live on the most—chaos or peace? Why?

CHAPTER 7

The Spell of Emotions

"Never let your excuses terrorize your dreams."

"Help! I can't even bring myself to get out of bed." That's how the conversation began. "My husband is in love with another woman!" she wailed. "He has left the house and moved in with her! I'm left alone with the kids and all the bills! YOU HAVE TO TELL ME WHAT TO DO!" It was a sad scenario for sure. She was in my congregation and coming to me for advice and direction in the middle of her crisis. It surely looked as though all her dreams for her marriage had sailed off into oblivion. No matter how much I tried to encourage her and offer advice, my words seemed to fall on deaf ears.

You no longer have to live jaded by your emotions.

Have you ever talked with someone so overwhelmed with emotional crisis that all potential hope for anything good appears at a total loss? No matter how hard you encourage them or talk sense to them, every piece of advice is **jaded** by the crisis at hand. It's as if a spell has taken hold. A debilitating grip of emotion now lords over every realm of their existence. You try and try again to help, but it seems no progress is ever made. How can this be? How can you give countless energy and time to help someone you love, only to witness him or her go off and do the opposite of every piece of advice you offered? How can doing what's right seem so clear to one person, yet so jaded and cloudy to another? Frustrating, isn't it? Let me ask you this:

Have you ever felt so overwhelmed by an emotion that it jaded how you perceived your situation?

Have you ever been so angry that it ruined your day?

Have you ever had a bout with jealousy that hurt a relationship?

Have you ever found it hard to forgive a person who severely wounded you?

If you answered "yes" to any of these questions, then you can see the power emotions have over life. Actually, emotions are hypnotizing. It can be a sunny and cloudless day, yet you can feel gloomy and drab inside.

Emotions are spellbinding.

It's why the teenage girl feels the need to cut herself. She's under an emotional spell. It's why the young boy keeps obsessively turning to porn to ease his lust. He's under a spell. It's why the mother left her husband and children to run off with her lover. She's under a spell. It's why the daughter has run to multiple men for approval and validation that she lacked from a father. She's under a spell. Why does the dad keep running to his addiction and skirting his responsibilities as a husband and a father? The spell has taken him captive. Why does the wife have one affair after another? She's under the spell of her emotions. Why does the meth addict keep chasing the buzz? It's all the same "reasoning." They all have been **hypnotized** by their emotions, and their emotions are dictating their choices.

To be hypnotized by emotions is crippling. It's crippling because it gives precedence to excuse making. Rather than pressing toward making things better, we make excuses for being **mediocre**. It's actually fairly easy to tell when our emotions have us captivated under their spell. It's easy to recognize when you've been hypnotized by your emotions. Just listen for the excuses. When excuses are made, the spell is cast.

When you end up making excuses for the way things are, you are under the spell of your emotions.

When we are hypnotized by our emotions, we will never see the need or reason to change. This by its very definition is dysfunction. It produces the inability to change because my emotional needs become my excuses. Ouch! My emotional needs become my excuses? That realization may sting a bit. When I do not deal with my poor emotional habits and continually make excuses, dysfunction becomes my norm. I become trapped in an endless cycle of emotional chaos that dissolves any residue of hope and affects my destiny. Chaos becomes my normal. I make **excuses** for my **chaos**.

The hypnotic spell of emotions:
"I am where I am, but it's not my fault!"

I saw the power of emotional chaos when a girl we'll call Mary walked into my office, tears filling her eyes, and proclaimed, "I throw up after I eat!" After a brief conversation, it became increasingly evident that Mary's emotions had her under a hypnotic spell. She couldn't have weighed more than 105 pounds, but Mary declared herself as "grotesquely fat." *How*, I thought, *could she see herself as fat?* But the web was spun. Every time she ate, she made an excuse to throw up. Her thoughts continuously focused on NOT being thin enough. Not looking thin enough became Mary's excuse to accept the detrimental habit of throwing up. This bred in her a consistent pattern of negative thinking about food. Food became "bad." Her perception that food was bad led to the warped reality that the worst thing she could do was eat. The warped perception "I'm fat and food is evil" dominated her life. Her emotional chaos (I feel fat) was the basis of her excuse (I must throw up). She was hypnotized by her emotions. She was **duped** by misguided feelings and thoughts.

That's how the spell begins. A negative thought begins to ravage your mind. If you tolerate it long enough, it affects your emotional stability. If you don't stop the negative patterns of thinking, you will soon have to make excuses in order to embrace those thoughts. And once you begin to make excuses, making progress toward your best life becomes arrested. Once you tolerate excuse making, failure is imminent. Almost every person I've met who cannot seem to make headway in life has a laundry list of excuses. There are always people, reasons, issues, stories, and drama linked to every excuse.

**It's hard to move forward in life when
every car hooked to your train
is loaded up with excuses.**

Let me share with you how excuse making played out on a daily basis in my life. I was pounded with thoughts of fear and death every time I would lie down at night. My mind would say, *What if one of my girls dies tonight in her sleep? What if I have cancer? What if Robbyn has an accident tomorrow? What if I die young and never see my kids grow up?* I remember one Sunday preaching a message in a church service and simultaneously struggling with the thought, *Please don't let me die here in front of all these people!* I recall an occasion when I burst into tears when Robbyn returned home late from an errand and forgot to call me. And I especially dreaded calls from unknown numbers, thinking as I answered the phone, *What if this call is about to be my Monica experience all over again?*

I have to admit, I was great at recognizing my issue. I just didn't do anything about it. Rather than tackling my negative thinking head-on I just tolerated it as normal. That brings me to share with you this profound truth: *What you tolerate becomes your normal.* If you keep tolerating the mess, then the mess will become your normal. If you keep tolerating the negative thoughts, then negative thoughts will be your normal. Tolerate anger, then anger will be your normal. Tolerate anxiety, then anxiety will be your normal. Tolerate pouting, then pouting will be your normal. I would have told anyone that I *hated* fear and certainly did not welcome any part of it into my life. However, by *tolerating* the fear, I was accepting its power over my life. So rather than hitting the issue head-on, I made excuses to avoid it.

To be hypnotized by your emotions is to tolerate your excuses.

Are you being hypnotized? Are you tolerating excuses for the mess you're in? Do negative emotions dominate every crisis you face? If your life is dominated by out-of-control emotions and excuse making, you are under the spell. Chaos and frustration will rule your day. Sadly, the mess will remain with you until you take responsibility. I have found that if you want to achieve a happy life, you must not let your excuses sabotage your success. Excuses rob your dreams and fuel your nightmares.

Ask yourself this question: "Have my dreams been sidetracked by my excuses?" The death of your **dreams** can be an excruciatingly painful experience. Such disappointment can cause you to throw in the towel. Know this: *Any excuse you tolerate will terrorize your dreams.* Rarely do people rob you of your dreams. More than likely, it's not the devil to blame. The death of one's dreams is usually due to a self-inflicted wound. Most often, we kill our dreams via our own tolerance of excuse making. When excuses become the dominating force in our lives, we will often settle for a mediocre life, rather than fighting for a satisfied life. We give up on our plan A and resolve to accept plan B instead.

It was a laundry list of excuses that nearly sideswiped my plan A—attending seminary to train for ministry. I feared writing papers. Seminary was a lot of writing. I hated to read. Seminary required loads of reading. I didn't want to leave the familiarity of all I loved. Seminary was one thousand miles from my present home. I had a great job as a youth pastor. Seminary would force me to leave my profession behind. I was able to live on a youth pastor's salary. Seminary cost more than I could afford. My excuses showed up at every bump in the road. Nevertheless, I shut down the rationale of every excuse and enrolled at Oral Roberts University. I killed off the excuses in order reach my dream.

Stop giving your excuses permission to sabotage your life.

Have your dreams been derailed by your mess? Are you making excuses for a mediocre life? Even though your dreams may have succumbed to some seemingly rational excuse, you can kill the excuse right now. You don't have to let your emotional mess encourage your excuse making any longer. You can still reach your greatest **potential**. Furthermore, you don't have to allow all the excuses that come through hurts, disappointments, anxieties, fears, frustration, unanswered prayers, or past experiences ransack the potential of your original dreams. Don't let your lifelong dreams succumb to the nightmare of your excuses. The tensions and frustrations you may be facing at present don't have the final say-so on the original plan for your life. Press into greatness. Don't settle for plan B because some crazy excuse has you thinking plan A is impossible.

I can truly say, "I've been there, done that." I've tasted the chaos and dysfunction of my own excuses. My excuses kept me paralyzed to progress. But I chose to quit making excuses. I quit settling for plan B. I decided to run headlong toward plan A, regardless of effort, cost, comfort, or reason. I chose to believe that all things were **possible**. I chose to live out my dreams rather than tolerate my excuses. I chose to settle things once and for all. I would no longer, ever again, be governed by my fears or excuses.

Perhaps you're a professional excuse maker. You may feel as though your dreams and destiny are eluding you. You may feel that you've already blown it so badly that there is no getting better. A word of advice: *Never let your dreams sleep in the coffin of your excuses.* Excuses will lull you to sleep and then proceed to suck the life right out of you. Tolerate excuses and you will never rise above your present condition. Your life will only trek along aimlessly on the path of frustration. Excuse making is a drip in the leaky faucet. Over time, it will create a mess in your head. Peace will avert you. Freedom will sidestep you. Success will elude you.

Shut down the voice of your excuses and you will be well on your way to an incredible life.

Break the spell. You don't have to give up or give in. Your excuses no longer need to define you. Don't lose sight of the dream God has given you for a better life. Don't settle for plan B. Don't become so overwhelmed by turmoil and disappointments that you feel defeated. Don't let the tragedies of your past dictate the decisions of your future.

Settle it for yourself by assuming responsibility for the mess in your head. Don't cast blame on other people. It's nobody else's fault. Settle it. Really, settle it at this very moment. NO MORE EXCUSES. People, money, time, crisis, family, health—NO MORE EXCUSES. Start believing that you are **no longer bound** by excuses. Give them no more place in your vocabulary. Stop allowing excuses to sidetrack your dreams. You can overcome. You can dream again. You can be happy again. An incredible life awaits you.

**You can have a better tomorrow if you simply
STOP MAKING EXCUSES.**

Chapter 7 Reality Check

1. What's your excuse?

2. How do you think excuse making hypnotizes you?

3. Why does it seem easier to embrace the excuse than fight for your dream?

4. Are you settling for a plan B in an area of your life? Why does plan B often seem easier than plan A?

5. Are you making excuses for mediocre?

6. Do you have a go-to excuse every time things get bad?

7. How do excuses sabotage your life?

8. How does this phrase impact your freedom: "I am where I am, but it's not my fault"?

9. "It's hard to move forward when every car hooked to your train is loaded with excuses." Why is this true?

10. On a sheet of paper, list all your excuses. Now crumble that sheet of paper and flush it down the toilet. Resolve to STOP making those excuses.

CHAPTER 8

"What If?"

"Why be afraid of the unknown? It's unknown."

"Dude, you gotta help me. I'm falling apart. I think I'm losing my mind. I think I'm going nuts." After several hours of talking with the man who had come to me desperate for help, I had to concur. He did seem to be losing his mind. He exhibited all the signs of someone who was falling apart. He was hopeless, distraught, negative, nervous, and not sleeping, and his thoughts were a whirlwind of chaos. The strange thing is that he wasn't facing a life-threatening crisis. He hadn't been diagnosed with a terminal disease. His house was not in foreclosure. His car was not about to be repossessed. No one whom he loved had recently passed away. What it all boiled down to was a girlfriend problem. There was a terrible, tangled mess in his head and it was all connected to relationship issues.

Most of our conversation was one sided. The man with the mess did all the talking. He was confident he loved his girlfriend, but his emotions were keeping him tormented with all the "**unknowns**." It wasn't the known variables that were robbing him of joy. It was the unknown questions he couldn't figure out. WHAT IF she's not the right woman? WHAT IF I'm just supposed to be a single man? WHAT IF she isn't ready? WHAT IF she says no when I propose? WHAT IF we can't afford to get married? WHAT IF it ends in divorce like my first marriage? He was tormented for sure. He was so focused on the "WHAT IF?" that he couldn't even enjoy what was currently good.

It was evident to me that he was deeply in love. However, rather than just resting in the fact that both he and his girlfriend were equally committed to each other, he was consumed with the unknown variables that come with any relationship. Rather than moving forward with good premarital counseling, he just kept asking himself, "WHAT IF? WHAT IF? WHAT IF?" He spent hours of unproductive energy miring through his mess. It was exhausting to be in the room with him. Embrace this: *It takes more emotional and physical energy to ponder "WHAT IF?" than it does to tackle a problem head-on.*

"WHAT IF?" scenarios are the emotional frustrations of trying to figure out what you can't figure out.

It's so easy to get lured into the trap of giving all your mental energy to the unknown variables you are facing. I call these unknown variables "WHAT IF?" scenarios. "WHAT IF?" scenarios are emotionally frustrating. I wish I had a dollar bill for all the hours I spent trying to figure out what I couldn't figure out. I could retire a fairly wealthy man. How does it make you feel when every ounce of your mental fortitude is spent trying to figure out what you can't figure out? You don't enjoy the life you have because you're focused on all the things, people, and circumstances connected to your mess.

I have found in my times of mess it's easier to role-play all the possible outcomes in my mind than face them head-on and formulate a game plan. However, I can assure you that *you can't endure the unknowns of life by role-playing outcomes.* I've played the "WHAT IF?" game like a professional. WHAT IF I die? WHAT IF Robbyn has a car wreck like Monica? WHAT IF one of my girls gets deathly ill? I was an expert at the game of "WHAT IF?"

"WHAT IF?" is a time waster, an energy drainer, and a dream killer.

Why would you ever want to focus on the unknowns? They are unknown. When you focus on unknown variables, it's disheartening. It's a hope robber. So why do we do it? Why do we drain every ounce of energy from our day to ponder the unknowns? Does focusing on all your unknowns make you feel any better? So why obsess over what is unknown? I wish I could give you the answers to all your life's "WHAT IFS?" The simple truth I've learned is that it takes faith not to be swamped by all the variables you can't figure out. The sure way to ending the terrorizing "WHAT IFS?" of your life is this: *Learn to trust in God.* You must focus on trusting God rather than figuring it all out. Having faith means you're willing to admit "I don't have it all figured out, but I will trust God anyway."

Entertaining your "WHAT IFS?" becomes the breeding ground for an emotional mess. It's just another drip in the leaky faucet that creates a torrential flood in your head. If you can **retrain** yourself to focus on what you DO KNOW and turn loose of what you DON'T KNOW, the dripping stops. The moment you let your UNKNOWNS rest in the hands of God, you can get busy *living* life out rather than *figuring* life out. Do you want to take a step toward a better life? Stop wasting your energy on the UNKNOWNS and start focusing your attention on the KNOWNS.

UNKNOWN: I have no idea how I will handle tomorrow.
KNOWN: God will take care of all things concerning tomorrow if I seek Him first.

UKNOWN: I just don't know how to make the right decision.
KNOWN: If I lack wisdom, I will ask God and He will give it liberally.

UNKOWN: What if I get fired from the job I love?
KNOWN: God works all things together for my good.

UNKNOWN: Will I survive this cancer?
KNOWN: Jesus took my infirmities and bore my sicknesses.

UNKNOWN: What if I never lose this weight?
KNOWN: I can do something every day to make progress.

UNKNOWN: I don't know if my marriage will ever work out.
KNOWN: I'm alive and breathing, so I'm going to enjoy my day.

UNKNOWN: What if my daughter gets hurt at gymnastics and breaks her arm?

KNOWN: She sure does love the floor routine, so the reward outweighs the risk.

UNKOWN: What if I flunk this exam?
KNOWN: I studied and gave it my best. If I fail, I'll just take it again.

UNKOWN: What if I miss God by stepping out?
KNOWN: He's a big-enough God to take care of me even if I miss Him.

Our human nature makes it so easy to get sucked into focusing on the unknowns in our lives. When you keep your thoughts on trying to solve the unknowns, frustration is the certain outcome. If frustration is the only outcome, then why are we so intent on playing the "WHAT IF?" game?

For example, when you are uncertain about the situation's outcome, you play the game. "WHAT IF?" momentarily calms the anxiety by offering you an acceptable and tolerable outcome. The upside? You find momentary peace. The downside? Rarely, if ever, does it work out like you imagined. When you tolerate "WHAT IFS?" at the beginning of every crisis, you will be on a constant roller-coaster ride of emotions. And any time you ride the emotional roller coaster, you get no closer to any certainty of a good life.

Try this emotional "WHAT IF?" test. Read the following sentences aloud:

WHAT IF I get cancer?
WHAT IF my husband is cheating?
WHAT IF my wife leaves me?
WHAT IF I lose my best friend?
WHAT IF I never conquer my depression?
WHAT IF I never find true love?
WHAT IF I can't ever get out of this looming debt?
WHAT IF I lose my house?
WHAT IF I can't forget what's been done to me?
WHAT IF I never get past the abuse?
WHAT IF I get fired?
WHAT IF I never get over being molested?

WHAT IF I'm never able to break free from my emotional mess?
WHAT IF I've blown it so badly that I can't ever get back to normal?
WHAT IF I'm just forever stuck on plan B?

How did those "WHAT IF?" scenarios make you feel? Do you see how discouraging "WHAT IF?" can be? Every question becomes emotionally defeating and energy draining. It's just never fun having to ponder all the unknowns of life. When we get **trapped** into putting "WHAT IF?" at the beginning of every sentence, the outcome will result in frustration and further misery.

Now try this emotional test. Read the following statements aloud:

DO YOU KNOW God is a healer of diseases?
DO YOU KNOW God can restore any broken relationship?
DO YOU KNOW God can bring you out of any tormenting lifestyle?
DO YOU KNOW He can solve problems that go beyond your wildest imagination?
DO YOU KNOW He can heal you from any hurt?
DO YOU KNOW God can forgive and redeem any mistake or failure?
DO YOU KNOW your dreams are still possible?
DO YOU KNOW God can bless you with a new job?
DO YOU KNOW you are a child of God and have His favor on your side?
DO YOU KNOW God is not sweating your situation right now?
DO YOU KNOW that God who controls the universe watches out for you?
DO YOU KNOW that possessions are not as valuable as your joy and peace?
DO YOU KOW that your plan A is still possible?

Notice a difference in your emotional state now? This can be a startling discovery when you have focused on the unknowns in your mess for so long. Faith starts to rise after reading one simple truth. "WHAT IFS?" were removed from the beginning of each sentence. I simply replaced all the unknowns with the known.

"WHAT IF?" is dangerous mental habit to tolerate.

I know it's hard to stop playing "WHAT IF?" in your head. It strategically postpones your reality. When you answer one "WHAT IF?" it only solicits further "WHAT IFS?" It merely takes you from one level of uncertainty to the next. Before long, "WHAT IF?" becomes your normal response, and you become **fixated** on mentally "fixing" it. But in reality, nothing ever gets fixed. Doubt creeps in. Prayers feel unanswered. You become worn out. All certainty is lost, and fixing your mess seems hopeless. And voilà! One day you wake up and you've settled for plan B.

One thing remains certain when entertaining "WHAT IF?" scenarios and that is "NOTHING is ever certain." Write this down: *NO CERTAINTY = A MESS IN YOUR HEAD.* "WHAT IF?" may start out feeling like you're going somewhere, but it will lead you down a dead-end street. You lose hope for any future good when you dwell on all the stuff you can't figure out. You'll wear yourself out trying to figure out all the answers, schemes, scenarios, and remedies.

You can train yourself to live beyond "WHAT IF?"

Ultimately, you have to learn how to **live beyond** "WHAT IF?" to end the mess in your head. There may be some uncertainties staring you in the face right now. Nevertheless, I want to give you some hope. Freedom is certain. Faith is certain. Trust is certain. Truth is certain. Remember, if you are breathing, **hope is certain**. So take a deep breath. As you inhale, take that as God's reminder that there is still hope. As you exhale, know that's His reminder you are one step closer to your next breath of hope. So rather than bemoaning the unknown, breathe in the known. Why not take a few minutes and just enjoy some good deep breaths of hope. I remind myself daily, "If I'm breathing, there's hope." Would you be willing to replace all of your "WHAT IFS?" with "DO YOU KNOWS?" Are you ready to put an end to all the frustrations of your unknowns? Are you ready to embrace a life filled with hopefulness? God has great plans for you. He has in store for you your best life ever.

When you end the "WHAT IFS?" you are well on your way to ending the mess in your head.

Chapter 8 Reality Check

1. Are you facing uncertainties in life now where you rehearse every possible outcome in your mind? How has this behavior helped or hindered you?

2. What is the end result of every "WHAT IF?" you play in your mind? Fear? Frustration?

3. Do you find yourself playing scenarios of possible outcomes more often than focusing on the promises that God gives about your situation? Why?

4. Which is easier—playing all the scenarios of possible outcomes in your head or letting go of what is unknown and trusting God? Why?

5. Are you willing to let go of the things you can't control and trust God to bring about the result? If so, what does that step of faith look like?

6. What if you removed all the "WHAT IFS?" from the crisis facing you right now? What differences would you notice?

7. Make a list of UNKNOWNS. Now, beside that list, write a column of things you are CERTAIN about—that is, the KNOWNS. Look at both columns. Which list brings you the most hope?

8. Why is the "WHAT IF?" scenario so dangerous to your emotional freedom?

Faith Exercise

Step one: Write your "WHAT IF?" on a small piece of paper.
Step two: Stare at what you've written, and speak to that unknown variable. Say, "I will conquer you." Don't be afraid anymore.
Step three: Fold the paper. Put it in your hands and pray this prayer:

Heavenly Father,
I am done fretting, worrying, and obsess-
ing over the things I can't figure out.
Today, I am making a conscious decision to let this "WHAT IF" go.
I will concern myself with it no more.
It is an UNKNOWN in my life and I choose to dwell on it no more.
I give it into Your care and I make a choice to trust You
to bring about my best life ever. In Jesus' name, so be it.

Step four: NOW TAKE THAT PIECE OF PAPER AND THROW IT IN THE TRASH.

CHAPTER 9

Help! I'm Addicted to My Emotions

"Never forfeit your future for your feelings."

After a few minutes of casually chatting in my office, he shocked me by blurting out, "I'm addicted to masturbating. I can't quit! I've tried for years to break the habit, but I just can't! It makes me feel so empty and useless, and I don't know what to do!" I hoped the shock I'd felt didn't show on my face. It was the first time anyone had openly confessed to me to being addicted to this sort of behavior. Because of his addiction, this man went on to disclose that he was tormented and guilt ridden, and the behavior was now affecting his sex life in his marriage. Clearly, his addiction to lustful images and the resulting behavior was ruining the betterment of his life.

Nobody ever wants to admit to being addicted to anything.

"Hi, I'm Mark, and I'm an addict." That kind of statement sounds so demeaning and damning. It must have been awkward for the man to confess his addiction to masturbation and all the dysfunctions that were part of his lifestyle. It seems like it would have been easier for him to have admitted, "Yeah, I struggle with masturbation." But to say the word *addicted*—that is pretty telling of one's emotional state. In reality, our emotions are so powerful they can cause us to become addicted to the very feelings we hate. Feelings may not hold a high percentage of certainty, but feelings are 100 percent addictive. Admittedly, we all have weaknesses. We all have issues and struggles. And yes, we'd all like to avoid the ultimate confession of being addicted to anything. However, when you avoid admitting to your addictions and instead label them as "issues" or "weaknesses," you only postpone the disastrous consequences that await you.

It's hard to call something an addiction when it pertains to one's own demise. I mean, when someone's overweight by a hundred pounds, it's hard for him or her to say, "I'm addicted to food." It's easier to confess, "Yeah, I struggle with my weight." The innocuous statement of "I love keeping up with my friends" is much better perceived than "I'm addicted to social media." The mainstream concept that there's "nothing wrong with admiring a pretty female" can keep a man from admitting, "I'm addicted to lusting after women." Usually, when we are dealing with our own personal demons, it's easier to **label** what's destroying us as anything other than an ADDICTION.

A perfect example of personal weakness can be found if we recall January 26, 1998, that moment when President Bill Clinton stated, "I want to say one thing to the American people. I want you to listen to me. I'm going to say this again: I did not have sexual relations with that woman, Miss Lewinsky." What a monumental day in American history when we hotly debated President Clinton's personal weakness. His weakness was splashed across the country in newsrooms, boardrooms, pulpits, and auditoriums. Was President Clinton's sex scandal a weakness or an addiction? We may never know. But as a country, we came to tolerate his behavior. My point? It's always **easier** to tolerate behavior when we acknowledge our emotional demons as weaknesses rather than as addictions.

Has your weakness become your addiction?

So what is the difference between a weakness and an addiction? Is one more potent than the other? How long does it take before a weakness becomes an addiction? One occurrence, one instance, or one lapse in judgment doesn't necessarily make us an addict to our behaviors, does it? At what point in time can we label our weakness as our addiction? Two times? Three times? After a month? Perhaps after a year? Is there ever a particular moment in time when my weakness becomes my addiction? Is it after one marital indiscretion? Two affairs? Is it after one drunken episode? Or after two or three DUIs? Is it after one full-blown temper tantrum? Or after you finally punch your spouse?

When we use the label of weakness, it removes the sting of the devastating effects of addiction.

Here's something to ponder to help you know why we like to use the label *weakness* rather than *addiction*. When I call my issue a weakness, it lets me feel as if I have some kind of **control**. Label my issue as an addiction, and I am stating I've lost control. And it sure feels better to tolerate a weakness than it does to own up to an addiction. Why? Because an addiction says, "I'm no longer in control." Truly, addiction is about control. If it's an emotion that controls me, then I am addicted to that emotion. If I blow my fuse every time life doesn't go as planned, I don't have a "short fuse"; I have an anger addiction. If I am undressing women with my eyes every time they walk into the room, I have an addiction to lust. The thing that separates a weakness from an addiction is its power to control me.

Being addicted to emotions is one of the greatest crises we face in our nation.

How many people do you know who are addicts to their emotions? How many people do you know live governed by their emotions rather than by their Creator? How many times have you seen emotions in control of a human rather than a human in control of his or her emotions? Morals and values are governed by emotions rather than absolutes. An entire generation has fallen prey to what FEELS right rather than what IS right. To emphasize this point, I am going to borrow a passage from Thomas Jefferson.

We hold these truths to be self-evident, that all men are created equal, that they are endowed by their Creator with certain unalienable Rights, that among these are Life, Liberty and the pursuit of Happiness. That to secure these rights, Governments are instituted among Men, deriving their just powers from the consent of the governed, That whenever any Form of Government becomes

destructive of these ends, it is the Right of the People to alter or to abolish it, and to institute new Government, laying its foundation on such principles and organizing its powers in such form, as to them shall seem most likely to affect their Safety and Happiness.
—Thomas Jefferson, US Declaration of Independence

Some of the most famous words of all time, these statements were heralded as a precise definition of human rights. However, consider the simple phrase, "We hold these truths to be SELF-EVIDENT." That's a wonderful thought until it becomes apparent that truth may no longer be deemed as "self-evident." That truth no longer derives its value from the Creator but from our emotions is a serious crisis we Americans face.

We are now a nation that formulates truth derived from our feelings.

Make mental notes about the changes you see around you: political, religious, economic, martial, sexual, and social. Our Creator is most certainly not dictating the changes you are witnessing. Our God, our Creator, the giver of Truth, does not govern most hearts. Instead, He has been **replaced** by feelings and desires. Emotion now sits on the throne of what is considered to be just and true. Read President Jefferson's words again. Let them soak into your mind. Now let me paraphrase one portion: 'If the government doesn't secure these rights and becomes destructive toward such end, abolish it, tear it down, and make a new government."

That's a bold statement. Perhaps the self-evident truth facing us today is that we are in dire need of a **course correction**—learning how to abolish and tear down the emotions that are destroying us. Feelings are governing our values, morals, decisions, laws, and justice. Feelings drive our marital choices, sexual desire, and sexual orientation. We are a nation addicted to our emotions. To clean up our personal mess, *we need to **abolish** the emotions that are destructive and establish a new government over our lives.* We must choose to be governed by God rather than addicted to our emotions. And that's the deal breaker between peace and an emotional mess: we can be governed by emotions, or we can be governed by God's Truth.

**You can be governed by God's Truth or
fall prey to your addictions.**

Here's how you fall prey to emotional addiction. It can happen rather quickly. Let's say a young boy makes a decision to look at a picture of a naked girl. Perhaps he saw it by mistake while surfing the web. Perhaps his girlfriend sexted the photo to him. It matters not how he got the picture. What matters is the rush of feelings the picture solicited. His emotions are set on fire. He stares. He lusts. He imagines. He's aroused. He masturbates. He feels relieved. Euphoric feelings leave him wanting more. **More. More. More.** The faucet starts to leak—*DRIP! DRIP! DRIP!* My, what a mess he will find himself in if he doesn't learn to conquer the rush of euphoric emotion.

The question we must ask is, "Is the young boy, by looking at one photo, an addict?" No, he's probably not a porn addict. However, a critical mishap has occurred. The young fellow has tasted the rush of his own emotions. What has taken place is an open doorway to emotional addiction. He might not yet be addicted to pornography, but you can be certain he's addicted to the feelings. With one picture and one flood of desire, an emotional drip was started. With one drip after another, he starts falling in love with his emotions. His emotions have been ignited, and if not controlled, a raging fire will burn. That first euphoric emotion becomes a spark that ignites a full-fledged raging fire of addiction if not properly contained.

**When you enter into a love affair with your emotions,
it will hinder everything good in your life.**

Here's a quote for you: "The habits you tolerate become the addictions that dominate." If you tolerate anger every time you face a crisis, anger will dominate you. You are no longer dominated by your dreams. You are now dominated by your anger. It's how addiction works. Addiction works to dominate us. Every emotional addiction that dominates me will become a death sentence to my dreams. When my choices are dominated by my emotions, I am destined to fail.

Let me explain how emotional addictions have worked in my own life. Emotionally, I am a "runner" and a "pouter." I hate confrontation. I loathe tense settings. I don't argue. I never cuss. I don't scream and holler. Nope. I just run, avoid, and usually wind up pouting. I hate tension and confrontation so much that I will just walk away and avoid it at all cost. So, my addictive behavior in a tense moment was to run. Running comforted me. Avoiding the tension soothed my soul.

However, as with all emotional addictions, the **end result** was never good. I usually ended up more tense than ever because nothing ever seemed to be resolved or worked out. I carried around a load of burden because I never got anything off my chest. I chose to run and avoid confrontation. Many a time I've lied to myself thinking that silent pouting is a far better strategy than getting angry. Truth be known, neither is better. Pouting is just as detrimental as an angry outburst. In the end, both carry the same devastating effect: I'm an emotional mess. The sad truth is, I believed that the addicted behavior of running from tension was far better than my confronting an issue. It took me years to break the habit of running to hide in my happy place. Thank God I found freedom from being a runner and pouter.

We all have some form of an emotional habit that drives us to our **happy place**. Perhaps, like me, you are a silent pouter. Maybe, conversely, you go all out and lose it and pitch royal fits. Maybe you slam doors. Maybe you love the use of foul language to get your point across. Maybe making threats and intimidation is your comfort zone. Maybe you run and hide in the comfort of a gallon of ice cream or a double cheeseburger. I don't know what your go-to addiction may be, but I do know that emotional addictions will always hold you in the clutches of your comfort zone. If you want to break free from emotional addictions governing your every move, you must learn to adjust to making decisions that remove you from your place of **comfort**. This is why most people never truly find freedom. They cannot stick to their decision because they can't outlast their discomfort.

To find freedom, you have to conquer "uncomfortable."

I can attest to you that my own precious emotions HATE dealing with the uncomfortable. I love the PRESENT ME. We're best friends. When the FUTURE ME calls me to go higher, the PRESENT ME hates going along. It's easier to **give in** to present comforts than press toward future potential.

The PRESENT ME always wars with the FUTURE ME. In a crisis moment, it's easier to yield to the need for immediate emotional comfort than to press toward success. Saying no to that extra cookie or that new guitar is never pleasant for the PRESENT ME. I've realized I may have to face some uncomfortable moments with the PRESENT ME to enjoy the beautiful moments of the FUTURE ME. However, if the PRESENT ME continually beats up the FUTURE ME, I'm going to be spending my energy cleaning up a mess.

Let's look at this principle from a biblical rationale. The book of Exodus shows how emotional habits kept God's people locked into an old pattern of existence, a **coffin** of comfort. It's a tragic tale of human emotion trumping God's called destiny. God's people had just been released from several hundred years of slavery. God was bringing them into a new reality of His life. All they had to do was follow God's directives. But frustration set in and they found themselves in an emotional stupor. Their comfort level became their coffin.

> *1 Then the whole community of Israel set out from Elim and journeyed into the wilderness of Sin, between Elim and Mount Sinai. They arrived there on the fifteenth day of the second month, one month after leaving the land of Egypt. 2 There, too, the whole community of Israel complained about Moses and Aaron. 3 "If only the LORD had killed us back in Egypt," they moaned. "There we sat around pots filled with meat and ate all the bread we wanted. But now you have brought us into this wilderness to starve us all to death."*
> EXODUS 16:1–3 (NLT)

To move forward, your decisions must dominate your emotions.

God had performed great signs and wonders. He brought these people out from years of bondage and slavery. He was leading them into a land that flowed with milk and honey. But at a moment of crisis and in a moment of uncertainty, they reverted emotionally to the place they were comfortable. Their feelings overrode their destiny. Their emotions dominated their decisions. When your emotions dominate your decisions, it becomes easier to go **backward** (into slavery) than move forward toward freedom. Note Numbers 14:35 where it says, "In this wilderness they shall come to a full end, and there they shall die." In a moment of crisis, in a wilderness, their emotions became their destruction. The decision they made was tragic. Why? It was a decision governed by emotion. They felt it was easier to live in the present than press toward the future. Comfort had a louder voice than destiny and present emotion trumped future potential. The potential of their future was ruined by the emotional mess of their present. They decided to forfeit life in the promise land for death in the desert.

I've proven it time and time again. It's just easier to live for the PRESENT ME than the FUTURE ME. Why? The voice of comfort tends to be louder than the voice of my destiny. The PRESENT ME likes a tension-free and comfortable life. The FUTURE ME always seems to lose out because it takes effort and work, and that's not a comfortable alternative. The PRESENT ME is far more emotionally addicted than the FUTURE ME. The PRESENT ME wants it now. I want comfort now. I want solutions now. I want the answer now. I've realized to have a chance for a better life, the FUTURE ME must dominate the PRESENT ME.

Your PRESENT ME may be driven by comfort, but your FUTURE ME is driven by destiny.

I've learned now how to break free from emotional addictions. I live for the FUTURE ME rather than giving in to the PRESENT ME. I live for my destiny rather than for my comfort. I've learned how to turn down the volume on uncomfortable. I've learned how to win in the crisis by outlasting the uncomfortable. I've learned how to stick to my decisions even through uncomfortable times. In short, I'm learning to live my decisions rather than being dominated by my emotions—regardless of the work it takes.

That's how you overcome the addiction to your emotions. You learn to be OK with bringing discomfort to the PRESENT ME so the FUTURE ME will be satisfied and successful. You learn to be governed by God's Word rather than by emotions. It works. I'm living proof. Through many years of search- ing, I found the way to freedom. The FUTURE ME has to matter more than the PRESENT ME. Oh, what an ongoing battle it is! If you want to stop the mess in your head from robbing you of the beauty of your tomorrow, you must learn to live for the FUTURE YOU rather than giving in to the PRESENT

YOU. The FUTURE YOU is screaming to the PRESENT YOU, "Let go of the comfortable so you can reclaim your potential!" Your destiny awaits you.

Live by your decisions, not by your emotions.

Chapter 9 Reality Check

1. When do you think it's fair to remove the label from a weakness and call it an addiction—a week, a month, six months, a year? Why did you choose your answer?

2. What do you feel is the main difference between a weakness and an addiction?

3. Why is it easier to label something a weakness rather than an addiction?

4. Why are decisions governed by emotions so threatening to your freedom?

5. Describe any addictive behavior presently at work in your life. What are the results you see?

6. Do you spend more energy on the PRESENT YOU or on the FUTURE YOU? Write down what the PRESENT YOU looks like. Describe the emotions prevailing.

7. Make a list of how the FUTURE YOU will look. Note five ways you can move toward becoming the FUTURE YOU right now.

8. Do you struggle to stick to your goals when things get uncomfortable for you? Why?

9. Do you make a decision and then postpone it because it seems too hard? Why?

10. Are you comfortable with where you are now? Is this where you really want to be? What's holding you back from making changes?

CHAPTER 10
The Chocolate Chip Cookie Lie

"A hole is just a hole until you die and they bury you in it."

Years ago, we invited one of our daughters' friends to play at our home. As the day progressed, Robbyn baked the girls a batch of homemade chocolate chip cookies. The aroma filled the air. When the cookies came out of the oven, my wife said, "Two cookies per child, please." The house was alive with glee—temporarily. Once the sugar high wore off, the house again grew quiet.

Denial is never your friend.

After several minutes, I noticed the girls were not romping through the house giggling, and no noise was coming from the other room. To me, quiet always means something sinister is at hand. Then I heard something in the kitchen. Robbyn called out, and our four-year-old houseguest came around the corner. Chocolate chip cookie residue covered her face and hands. Robbyn asked the provocative question, "Have you eaten more than two cookies?" She quickly replied, "No, ma'am!" "Are you sure you haven't had any more cookies?" Robbyn asked again. "Yes, ma'am, I'm sure," she responded.

The next question honed in on her guilt: "Then why is there chocolate on your face and hands?" "There's no chocolate on my face!" the determined child said very matter-of-factly. "Then what's that chocolate stuff all over your face?" Robbyn again posed. Again the answer was stoic and certain: "There is no chocolate on my face. I didn't eat any cookies." So, Robbyn ended the fiasco with a gentle blow of humility: "Then let's go wash your face because you have something chocolaty all over it." They went to the kitchen to wash the mysterious substance from the small hands and face. When Robbyn returned to where I was sitting, she smiled and stated, "All the cookies have been eaten."

The risk of getting better is often silenced by denial.

Sadly, most people commit the "chocolate chip cookie lie" when facing an emotional crisis. The chocolate is on your face, yet you refuse to admit to having an issue. This is the chocolate chip cookie lie: *You avoid the inevitable and **deny** the obvious.* It's so easy to avoid. The drip is overlooked because the mess it is making isn't clearly obvious. But here's what's funny. Most people in your life recognize your drip before you do. Your emotional habits and addictions are usually obvious to all who come in contact with you. Why? We find more comfort in denial than in acceptance. Acceptance poses too great a risk.

Here's the deal. If you avoid the obvious, then the inevitable is failure. Mark this equation down: *Avoidance + Denial = Failure.* I can tell you this from my own life experiences: you can never overcome what you deny. You can't have chocolate all over your face and hope no one will notice. You can't move through life as if your mess doesn't exist. The answer to freedom lies in taking responsibility for the mess that's going on in your head.

Here's a truth that is vital to cleaning up the mess in your head. Denial doesn't eliminate disaster; it just postpones disaster. Denial has one goal in mind: disaster. Denial shifts the blame. Denial shirks responsibility. When you shift the blame onto anything other than yourself, success becomes nearly impossible. If you want to break free, you must learn how to assume the responsibility of putting an end to all the negative thoughts and emotions going on in your head.

To break free, you must assume responsibility.

Did you get that? You cannot find freedom while tolerating, accepting, and ignoring the effects of emotional addictions and habits. You have to take responsibility for your freedom. It may seem that you are where you are because of what's been done to you by another. But no more blaming people. No more blaming God. No more blaming your past. You can't afford to ignore it. Your emotions sit in the driver's seat. And sometimes that revelation can be a hard pill to swallow.

People and past circumstances don't rule your emotions; you do.

So let's start by assuming some personal responsibility. Are you angry? Then whom do you need to forgive? Are you overspending? Then will you stop using your credit cards? Are you insecure? Then will you leave your comfort zone and try something new? Are you scared to make a move for the better? Then will you step out and at least give it a try? Do you need to lose weight? Then are you willing to eat better and get busy with healthier habits? Is your marriage getting weaker and weaker? Then are you willing to open up and seek help? The ball is in your court. There's no one else to blame if you really want to move forward toward freedom. It starts with you and the decision you will make to own up to the poor habits that are trying to make a mess of your life.

Blaming someone else makes your mess messier.

I know it may seem difficult to come to terms with the idea that the ball is in your court. But really, one thing is certain: people can't rob your joy, happiness, or contentment. How can I say that people are not your problem? How can I say you can't blame another person when you are where you are because of another's actions? It's a simple deduction. People can't make you mad if you choose not to let them make you mad. Circumstances can't defeat you if you choose to not let circumstances defeat you. Take responsibility. Start by changing YOU first. Begin with your decisions, not someone else's. Take charge of your life.

It's easier to fight some external battle than defeat the internal battle of your own emotional torments. Fighting with yourself is more difficult than fighting the devil or another person. In an external fight, the blame can be shifted elsewhere and you can, at any time, escape the fight by ignoring it or simply walking away. But truly, how can you escape yourself? You can't.

Here's a truth I learned the hard way: I can't run from me. I can't hide from me. I can unfriend everyone on social media, but I cannot get rid of myself. I wake up with me. I lie down with me. I am **stuck** with me. Therefore, I am the beginning point of my freedom. How you handle *yourself* will be the starting point of *your* freedom. You must start with you. You must admit that your own emotions are to blame. Isn't it alarming how often we spend our energy fixing everyone else's problems while ignoring our own dripping faucet?

It's OK to admit, "It's me."

I finally took a look in the mirror. I admitted that fear was dominating me, and I was tired of it ruining my life. I admitted to the "cookie mess" that was clearly on my face, and I began to walk out to my freedom. So, if there is cookie residue on your face, it's time to admit that you ate the cookies. As stated above, "A hole is just a hole until they bury you in it." Don't ignore the obvious. Ignoring the obvious is a grave danger. No pun intended. Now clean up the mess, and get busy living. It's OK to **own it**. It's OK to admit, "It's me." Once you start with you, healing begins.

You certainly cannot control the actions and emotions of others, but you can **start** by controlling your own. Have you been hurt? You may never get an apology, but you can start by forgiving first. Your best friend may have betrayed you, but you can choose to bless him or her in return. You may never get your money back from the person who swindled you, but you can let go of the anger. You may not be able to reclaim your virginity, but you can let the shame of molestation/rape fall into the grace of God. You may not be able to save your marriage, but you can let go of the bitterness and find happiness again. You may never know the reason your parents abandoned you, but you can be grateful you are alive and now have the potential to show love to others.

You can't control every circumstance, but you can control every emotion.

Control is an illusion. I'm going to say that one more time: *You can't control every circumstance you face, but you can own the emotional response you make.* I wish we didn't have to deal with all the erratic emotions that come with living on this planet and dealing with life and people. However, emotions are with us from womb to tomb. That said, being ruled by your emotions does not have to be a normal part of living. You can win and overcome any emotion trying to control you.

Don't be lazy about fighting your way there. You must take responsibility. You must be willing to fight. You must go to battle. You must declare war on your out-of-control emotions. No one else holds the key, the pardon, or the release. Now is the time to stop shifting the blame and making excuses. You must stop blaming God, the devil, your spouse, your friend, or any other person you deem worthy of guilt.

Only you can examine your own soul and enthrone God as Ruler of your emotions. Tackle the chocolate chip cookie lie head-on. If there is a mess, assume responsibility. If you don't learn how to take responsibility, you will remain forever paralyzed under the deceptive spell of dysfunction. Let the possibility of **freedom** start brewing in your soul. Even though things may seem really unfair at this point in your journey, I am asking God to give you the courage to take responsibility. Look in the mirror, wipe off the cookie mess, stop ignoring, stop blaming, and begin to take steps toward freedom.

Your freedom starts by owning responsibility.

Chapter 10 Reality Check

1. Explain this: "Denial is never your friend."

2. Why does it seem easier to ignore or blame rather than take responsibility?

3. Why is taking responsibility such a key component to finding your freedom?

4. What is one thing you can do now to take responsibility?

5. Why does a decision to get better seem so risky?

6. Is there someone you've blamed that you may need to forgive right now? Will you? Do you find it difficult to make the first move toward forgiveness? Why?

7. Why does it seem unfair to take responsibility when you know it's not your fault?

8. How will you put this statement to practice in your life: "I can't control the actions and emotions of others, but I can start with controlling my own."

9. Looking at your present situation, is it easier to blame others for where you are or take responsibility for where you are? Explain.

10. Explain this phrase: *Avoidance + Denial = Failure*. List some ways you have avoided dealing with your mess.

CHAPTER 11

Emotional Poker

"Fighting emotion with emotion may not earn you a prison sentence, but it will earn you a lifetime of misery."

et me explain the game of emotional poker by sharing a life-defining moment I experienced in spring 1984. I was nineteen years old, playing softball for my local church team, and was slated to be the center fielder. Why on earth the coach decided to put a lazy-eyed, myopic player in centerfield I will never know. Despite my wall-eyed predicament, there I was, somewhere in the middle innings, standing in center field, and full well knowing the ball was about to come my way. I readied myself by doing what I had always done to prep for a fly ball: I closed my lazy eye and stared intently with my good eye to try focusing on the coming ball.

Before the pitch crossed the plate, I felt as if time stopped. My heart started to beat erratically. The voices in my head started shouting, "You are going to die on this field!" I felt as if the field was spinning. I couldn't focus. I was panicking. I started thinking to myself, *No! Not now! I can ignore this and it will go away.* I tried ignoring it. Didn't work. I tried refocusing my thoughts. Nothing. At that moment, while panicking in center field, I suddenly heard a voice speak to me in all my lazy-eyed wonder. It was clear and distinct, and it said, "You will never overcome this by ignoring it. I called you to fight, not to ignore."

You will never overcome your negative emotions by ignoring them.

This thought certainly didn't originate from my own mind: "You will never overcome this by ignoring it. I called you to fight, not to ignore." I had spent years trying to ignore the thoughts of dying, hoping they would go away. I had reasoned in my mind for years that I could just simply ignore thoughts and things would change. But I wasn't growing out of the hell I was experiencing; indeed, it was getting worse. Ignoring the death thoughts was a **mind trick** I played on myself to wish the horror away. The voice took me by surprise. Indeed, it unnerved me. "You will never overcome this by ignoring it. I called you to fight, not to ignore."

Suddenly, I began to rethink how to fight my emotional battle. I realized that I could no longer fight my emotions with my emotions. I could not fight fear by ignoring fear. I could no longer fight thoughts of dying by ignoring death. I was gaining awareness that my emotions were holding me **hostage**, mainly because I was trying to fight chaotic emotions with other chaotic emotions. It was as if I was playing a game of poker that I could never win. I realized that I had embraced the perception that one emotional hand of cards could win over another emotional hand of cards. It was a **fallacy** I'd come to completely believe in. And this line of thinking was dooming me to certain failure.

You cannot fight emotions with emotions and expect success.

This perception bound me to the belief that I could overcome one negative emotion with another equal, yet opposite, emotion. I literally believed I could win over fear by ignoring it. Here is what I learned after meditating on the truth from the voice that spoke to me on the softball field. You will never win the battle fighting one emotion with an equal, opposite emotion.

Fighting emotion with emotion is what I call **emotional poker**. Although it's easy to try to play emotional poker, you will never win the battle doing so.

You weren't created or designed to do life that way. If you don't stop, your only destination will be a cyclical pattern of bondage and temporary, fleeting relief. This emotional poker may seem beneficial as you trade one weaker emotion for another more desirable emotion; however, you will eventually succumb and fold under pressure.

Once you buy into the belief that emotional poker "works," your potential to move toward freedom becomes paralyzed. Any time you fight one emotional battle with the energy of other emotional decisions, you will remain in the cycle of dysfunction. You might play a different hand every time, but it's always the same game—and you will certainly lose at every hand you play. Fighting emotion with emotion will not earn you a prison sentence, but it will earn you a lifetime of misery.

**I found freedom when I put an end to
fighting emotion with emotion.**

One of my favorite stories proving the detrimental nature of emotional poker concerns King David in the Bible. It's a fairly familiar tale, known by most Christians and non-Christians alike. You can read all the dirty details in 2 Samuel:11 and 12. Both chapters give great insight into the demise of any who dare attempt to enter the game of emotional poker. The story is complete with David being dealt a very "risky" hand and outlines how he gambles with such. Let's take a look at David's hand.

First card: AVOIDANCE—Rather than going off to war to fight with his troops, David decides to stay home and relax.
Second card: LUST—Rather than relaxing (David while at home and not at war), leads with his second card: he lusts after a married woman bathing naked on a rooftop outside his window.
Third card: DENIAL—To satisfy his lust, David takes the third card and invites the naked, bathing, other man's wife to his lair.
Fourth card: SHIRK RESPONSIBILITY—Rather than simply wining and dining her, David takes the next card and has sex with the woman and gets her pregnant.

Fifth card: MURDER—Rather than being satisfied with sex, David decides to take this woman to be his wife. To do so takes his fifth and final card. This card is murder.

King David attempts to hold all five cards in his hand and stay in the game. What he has not factored into the equation is that God knows King David can't play these cards and remain true to his calling. The game comes to an abrupt end when David's emotional decisions are brought to light, and he now has to assume the responsibility of the mess he created. He is confronted with the spiritual decision of repentance. Will King David stay in the game? Or will he fold, call it quits, take responsibility, repent, and let God redeem the mess he created?

The same question holds true for all of us today. Will you stay in the game or will you fold? To end the game, you must repent. You must come to the realization that your out-of-whack emotional decisions will never leave you satisfied. Your emotional satisfaction will only come when God's will trumps every one of your poor emotional choices. That is the detriment of beginning the game of emotional poker in the first place. Once the game begins, it is a **downward spiral** until repentance ends the game. Make note that once the game begins, you will always be forced to keep the game in play to remain happy and content in your emotional state. Remember King David's story: an emotional decision that began by shirking responsibility on the sunlit balcony of the royal palace ended in murder via the darkened bedroom of adultery.

You will never win at the game of emotional poker.

Never! You will never win at emotional poker. Although it may feel as if each card dealt is just another rush of excitement and euphoria, the end result is never good. At every step along the way, each card being dealt to King David was a greater rush of emotion than the previous card he held in his hand. Lust was more valuable than relaxing. Sex was more valuable than lusting. Murder was more valuable than sex. Lying and hiding were more valuable than being condemned to death. Once you begin the game of emotional poker, you will always choose the hand that affords you the most comfort, ease, and pleasure.

The game will ruin friendships, marriages, and anything else you choose to gamble while playing.

Playing emotional games is a big gamble.

You can't fight disappointment with pouting. You can't fight pouting with whining. You can't fight whining with anger. You can't fight anger with resentment. You can't fight resentment with bitterness. Neither can you fight bitterness with revenge. You can't fight stress with smoking. Neither can you fight frustration with alcohol. You can't fight hurt with prescription meds. And you surely can't fight rejection with cutting. Bottom line: you can't fight emotion with emotion. Gambling with your emotions will end in certain defeat. Stop fighting emotional decisions with other emotional decisions. If you are going to win at the game of emotional poker, you do so by never entering the game in the first place. You must never move past the first card being dealt to you.

Emotional poker is akin to the guy who says, "Well, I may look at a woman other than my wife, but I would never sleep with her." In other words, one unacceptable emotional pattern is traded for another emotional pattern that is more acceptable. He's fighting emotion with emotion. He needs to get out of the game immediately by training his eyes not to even take a gander at any woman other than his wife. How about the woman who says, "I may be a jerk to my husband, but I am sweet and loving to my kids." She is playing the game of emotional poker. She justifies one negative emotional response by offsetting it with another acceptable response. Wouldn't it be better to just own the responsibility of being a jerk and make a decision to change for the better? At a glance, to change seems so much more difficult than remaining in the game. Change feels risky, while the game of emotional poker feels rewarding.

I can attest that emotional poker is far greater than risky. Emotional poker is deadly.

It was staring at me on my desk. A letter from prison addressed to me was waiting to be opened. I hadn't heard from this man in years. We had a long-term friendship and had done ministry together in years past. I never expected a handwritten letter from his prison cell. I knew he had a history of inner struggles, but he seemed to be just fine on the outside. I never imagined what I was about to read. It was beyond my wildest imagination. As I read, I was filled with great sorrow.

For as long as he could recall, this man had struggled with lust. The lust had grabbed hold over his mind through one perverted image. Just one image. That lust now had him in a spell. He couldn't seem to shake it. He ignored it. Denied it. Tolerated it. Accepted it. Over time, he believed the lust could be relieved through masturbation. He began playing emotional poker. He tolerated the lust by accepting masturbation as his remedy. The game had begun. The first card had been played, and it would continue through his teen and college years.

Finally, after marrying the love of his life, he thought he would find relief. However, marriage didn't cure his issue. The lust prevailed. Lust had become his addiction. Neither masturbation nor marriage was curing it. His emotional connection to masturbation was no longer helping. Sex in the marriage, regardless of how frequent, was not answering the emotional dysfunction now driven by his addiction to lust. Pornography came and went through the years. Sometimes he'd spend a month clean of pornography or masturbation and would feel a sense of freedom. Yet the lust always resurfaced. He simply couldn't shake the addiction, and he felt paralyzed to hope.

Never believe the lie, "It is what it is."

It was a true scenario of emotional poker. How so? He never took the appropriate steps to conquer the lust. The lust always prevailed. One greater emotion always trumped a lesser weaker emotion. He never got help. He never sought true relief. He resolved that he needed to conquer the mess in his head through emotions alone. Addictions were tolerated. Habits led to dysfunction. Perhaps guilt and shame kept him isolated from help. But the lust had become such a part of his life that it became his ultimate undoing. Hopelessness sunk its fangs deep in his soul. After years of lustful living, he gave up hope of ever finding freedom. He became paralyzed by hopelessness. And he succumbed to the lie, "Oh well, it is what it is."

What was the outcome of it all? What was the outcome of his tolerance? What was the outcome of his addiction? What was the outcome of his inability to take responsibility? What was the outcome of his emotional poker? He now sits in a prison cell found guilty of sexually molesting his foster son. His outcome? He's spending thirty years in a prison cell with no possibility of parole.

**Using emotion to fight emotion is a true sign
you are playing the game of emotional poker.**

You simply cannot substitute one emotion for another emotion to justify the end. It keeps you paralyzed because you spend all your energy ignoring one catastrophic emotion with another acceptable alternative emotion. Emotional poker. The sad part? You never win. The game is designed to keep you believing "you can do it" while sinking you deeper into an emotional mess. Like King David and his story, emotional poker will never show you the end result until you have to ultimately fold and bow out of the game. You lose.

Assess the battle you are in now. Are you fighting emotions with emotions? Are you fighting from the viewpoint of your emotional framework or are you fighting from your spiritual framework? Are you fighting anger by pouting? Are you fighting bitterness by ignoring it? I will teach you in the pages ahead how I learned to fight emotional addictions with spiritual certainty. For now, make a choice to start moving away from the paralysis of your perceptions. Choose to fight from spiritual absolutes rather than from emotional substitutes. Put an end to the game of emotional poker.

Focus on the absolute nature of God and His Word and not on the uncertainty of your emotional state of being. When you do this, you give yourself hope. **Hope** produces potential. Potential produces passion. Passion produces action. Action releases faith. Faith equals certainty. And finally, certainty is belief. Believing makes all things possible.

"What do you mean, 'If I can'?" Jesus asked.
"Anything is possible if a person believes."
MARK 9:23 (NLT)

The Holy Spirit wants to help you.

God has designed you to be an emotional creature. Your emotional being is God given and God designed. So in order for you to be functional on this planet, God had to give you a **remedy** for you to control your emotions. That remedy is His Word and His Spirit. He designed us to feel with emotion, but He commands us to live by His Spirit, and not by our feelings.

> *So I say, let the Holy Spirit guide your lives. Then you won't be doing what your sinful nature craves.*
> GALATIANS 5:16 (NLT)

If you want to see the possibility of coming out of your emotional mess, you must fight from a place of absolute spiritual certainty, not emotional uncertainty. You must fight your emotions with God's help. Don't play games with your emotions. Stop the game of emotional poker. Don't play. Fight. Fight with God's help. Fight by yielding to His Word. Fight with His power. Take a RISK to break free from the emotional mess that you've become so comfortable tolerating. You have to draw a line in the sand and put an end to the mess. Will you take that risk? Believe me, it's worth it.

You can conquer any out-of-control emotion with God's help.

Chapter 11 Reality Check

1. Explain this: "You will never overcome your negative emotions by ignoring them."

2. Do you find yourself playing emotional poker? Why?

3. Why does it seem so easy to fight emotions with emotions?

4. Are you finding it hard to move forward? Why? Do you feel stuck? Explain.

5. Why is emotional poker so appealing?

6. Why is emotional poker considered a deadly game?

7. If we can NEVER WIN at playing emotional poker, why do we often try so hard to stay in the game?

8. Is there any situation at present where you are playing emotional poker? What is it?

9. What role does the Holy Spirit play in helping you overcome the game of emotional poker?

10. Identify any emotions that are not succumbing to God's help. Over each out-of-control emotion, pray this prayer:

Heavenly Father,
I make a choice today, a decision of my will, to no longer
fight the battle of my emotions by appealing to alternative emotions.
I repent of trusting my emotions for my vic-
tory. Forgive me for relying and
dwelling on the uncertainties of the things I don't know. I now choose
to trust the One who is absolutely certain. I choose to trust You,
Heavenly Father. You are my new absolute and I trust Your grace
and Your Word for every emotional concern I have. Thank You
for Your freedom and for giving me the strength to overcome.
In Jesus's name, Amen.

CHAPTER 12
Your Line in the Sand

SCHWARTZ: *Well, I double–DOG dare ya!*

RALPHIE: *NOW it was serious. A double–dog dare. What else was there but a "triple dare you"? And then, the coup de grace of all dares: the sinister triple–dog dare.*

SCHWARTZ: *I TRIPLE–dog dare ya!*

RALPHIE: *Schwartz created a slight breach of etiquette by skipping the triple dare and going right for the throat!*

— *A CHRISMAS STORY* BY JEAN SHEPHERD

O h, the triple–dog dare. It's the line of demarcation in the sand. It's the defining moment determining your next move. Will you or won't you? This question, if we "dare" to entertain it, is the truth to ending the mess in your head. Will you or won't you draw a line in the sand to end it? A line that states, "Enough is enough. This mess stops now." You can't play with the mess in your head like it's your best friend. You fix the drip by drawing your line in the sand. "I triple–dog dare ya!" Taking a stand may seem scary, but it begs you to answer, "Will I or won't I?"

Your mess stops here and now regardless of how you feel.

It's not always easy to draw a line in the sand when your emotions are in play. Negative emotions and thoughts will always force you to compromise the line you've drawn. They want you to keep tolerating the mess in your head. The mess will go to bed in your head and wake up in your head—day in and day out until you stop it. Freedom begins by picking up a mental stick and drawing the line in the sand that announces to the mess in your head, "The buck stops **here** and **now**." Drawing a line in the sand says, "I no longer tolerate the mess." You arrest the mess by putting an end to the excuse of tolerating it.

My line in the sand ended a twenty-year drip that started in 1975 when I was ten years old. I can tell you that after two decades of a *DRIP! DRIP! DRIP!* I was a mess. But on July 31, 1995, all was about to change for the better. I was preparing for another evening of vacation Bible school (VBS). I was moments from walking on stage to perform when panic set it. A thought went off like a bombshell in my mind: *You will die in front of all these kids tonight.* I was in utter torment. I started losing control mentally. I began to beg God, *Please, please don't let me die in front of all these kids. Please, God, don't let me die.* The thought of dying and the feeling of panic wouldn't go away. I was in the middle of a full-on panic attack, but the show had to go on.

As soon as that night of VBS concluded, I ran down the hallway of the church and collapsed in my office chair. The room was spinning. I didn't know what to do. As I begged God to heal me, I gained enough composure to phone my mother. Feeling as if my world was caving in around me, I dialed her number. Our conversation was as follows:

"Mother?"

"Yes."

"I think I'm going to die!"

"DIE? What's wrong?"

"I can't breathe. The room is spinning, and I can't shake that thought that I am going to die!"

"Mark, you may be just going too hard and having your blood sugar dro—NO!"

It was one of the strangest moments of my life when I heard my mother yell, "NO!" I didn't know what was going on, but what she said next was a life-defining moment that caused me to draw my line in the sand. Here is what my mom prayed over the phone:

> "NO! I rebuke a spirit of fear and command fear to lose its hold over your life, your mind, and your future. Fear has no place, no right, no hold, nor has any power over you. Matthew 18:19 says, 'If two of us agree as touching any-thing it shall be done for them by the Father in heaven.'"

At that instant, I felt something leave my life. I was totally changed in a moment. What I had fought for the last twenty years was gone in a breath. HOPE came. I felt so free. My moment had arrived. Finally, I felt I had out-lasted the hell. I had overcome the torment. I had conquered the fear. It was a most glorious occasion. I felt as if I had been born again. I was *FREE! FREE!* Free from the *DRIP! DRIP! DRIP!* No more mess in my head—or so I thought.

It wasn't long before I bumped headlong into the *DRIP! DRIP! DRIP!* again. I had enjoyed twelve luxurious days torment-free—no mess in the head. In less than two weeks, I had returned to the gym, started running again, and was not wondering if death would conquer my life. Then, out of nowhere, it all came flooding back. The thoughts rushed in. *"You're not free!" DRIP! DRIP! DRIP!* The fear returned. *"You're still going to die!" DRIP! DRIP! DRIP!* The anxiety was back. The torment was back. Except this time, it didn't seem like a drip. It felt more like Niagara Falls. And I was drowning in a torrent of fearful thoughts. *DRIP! DRIP! DRIP!*

Refuse to give in to your feelings.

There was something, however, different about the fear and anxiety this time. The thoughts and fears were still real; I just didn't give in to them. I had done something on July 31 on the phone with my mother that I had never done before. Rather than hanging up the phone with my fingers crossed, hop-ing I would forever be free, I hung up the phone with a line drawn in the sand. The difference? My line in the sand stated, "The mess stops here and now regardless of how I feel." My line said I was determined to never let fear dominate me again. So on July 31, 1995 at 8:20 p.m., I drew a line in the sand once and for all, putting an end to my negative and fearful thinking. I changed my negative perceptions. I drew my line of freedom. I drew my line of hope. I refused to give in to my feelings. After twenty years of a mess, I drew a line of certain declaration: "The mess ends here and now, and fear will never follow me one day further."

On July 31, 1995, my life took a 180-degree turn. That turn came because of a decision to stop tolerating the mess. I wrote the following on an old yellow Post-it note to remind me of my line in the sand. It stated:

On
July 31, 1995,
8:20 p.m.,
120 Cornerstone Drive, Johnson City, Tennessee,
with my head on a blue Vine's Expository Dictionary
on the phone with my mother
based on Matthew 18:18–19,
I was delivered from a spirit of fear!

I carried that Post-it note everywhere. I kept it in my wallet. I rehearsed it every morning. I quoted it in the car. I said it during my prayer time. I said it in the bathroom, at the gym, and in the grocery store. I spoke it all the time, every day. I learned it backward and forward. So on day twelve, after my initial moment, when the fearful thoughts decided to return, I rolled down the windows of my car as I was riding down the highway, and I shouted the following:

On
July 31, 1995,
8:20 p.m.,
120 Cornerstone Drive, Johnson City, Tennessee,
with my head on a blue Vine's Expository Dictionary
on the phone with my mother
based on Matthew 18:18–19,
I was delivered from a spirit of fear!

I yelled it over and over again as I rode down the highway. I yelled it until the veins in my neck popped and my head felt as though it would burst. I refused to give in to all the thoughts of fear anymore. I kept rehearsing the truth. I am free! I am free! I am free! Not because I felt free but because

On
July 31, 1995,
8:20 p.m.,
120 Cornerstone Drive, Johnson City, Tennessee,
with my head on a blue Vine's Expository Dictionary
on the phone with my mother
based on Matthew 18:18–19,
I was delivered from a spirit of fear!

I didn't care what people thought. I didn't care if I was heard mumbling it to myself. The truth was in my bones. I got it in my soul. I got it in my head. I wasn't going to pout, run and hide, or seek another moment. I had my moment on July 31. My line in the sand had been drawn, and it brought me hope. Hope gave me faith. I wasn't going to cave in for some out-of-control thought of death or revert to some emotionally dysfunctional habit of negative thinking. Finally, there was an end to my mess. The end wasn't a feeling. The end was my line that shouted triumphantly, "The mess stops here!"

This may be difficult for some to grasp because they want freedom based on a feeling. However, the moment the mess returns, they tolerate and accept the mess. As soon as circumstances conflict with emotions, that familiar mess comes rushing back. As soon as emotions resurface, faith becomes buried. As a result, they assume freedom isn't real. They assume God doesn't care. They assume prayers weren't answered. They rationalize feelings over faith. And they resolve to keep living the cycle dominated by the mess.

Freedom is a fact, not a feeling.

Your line in the sand must be based on a decision and not a feeling. You don't draw the line because you feel free. You draw the line because you are free. Jesus has already promised you freedom—not because of who you are but because of what He's done. You're free now. Pick up the phone and call a friend who can agree with you and spur you on to hope. Whatever it takes, draw your line in the sand. Get out a Bible and ask God to reveal to you a Scripture of hope. When you feel hope rising, write down the time, the Scripture, the date, the decision you've made, and the person who has agreed with you. Your line in the sand is your faith that states you are already free—regardless of how you feel.

Negative thoughts will always try to fight you at the line of demarcation. Negative and hopeless thoughts pull you back to the line and keep you from progressing. If hopelessness can keep you from drawing the line, then you will most definitely live defeated. Why? Because you will forever be chasing a hope that is based on feelings rather than fact. But once you find hope based on faith and you settle your moment, you can begin to move forward. It's at this line in the sand where your freedom becomes a reality. From the time you draw the line in the sand, every new day takes you further past your mess. The line gives you hope that it *has* ended, not hope that it *might* end. It ended because you ended it. Period.

The moment you make a decision to believe is the day you draw your line in the sand.

Not long ago, a man in his twenties came to me struggling with porn and depression. He seemed well defeated. Even though he was relatively young, he had been struggling with such for years on end. He stated to me that he was about to go on a fast so he could get free. He then made the comment, "If this doesn't work, I don't know what I will do." I then assured him, "It's not going to work. The devil will make sure you don't get free if you are basing your freedom on something uncertain." So I offered him the advice of drawing his own line in the sand.

I asked him to find a Scripture—a certain verse that spoke to him. I asked him to believe the verse. I asked him to make a handwritten note marking the day and time he chose to believe the verse. I asked him to once and for all draw his line in the sand. I asked him to put an end to the lust and depression because of what he believed, not what he felt. I asked him to fight from a place of certainty. He was to remember the day he chose to believe. I asked him to stop fighting from a place of uncertainty and from what his feelings dictated to him.

Would you like to know the end result? Two weeks following our initial discussion of his struggle with porn and depression, he came to me and stated, "I found freedom. I found a verse in the Bible, and I drew a line in the sand. It stated, 'I set before you life and death—choose life.' So, I choose life." How awesome is that? "I choose life." He drew his line in the sand. He learned a great truth. Freedom came by choice, not by feeling. He found freedom by being certain, not fretting uncertainty.

I could share countless stories of friends over the years who have all drawn their lines in the sand and it worked. Yes, it **really** worked. They found freedom. So, will you? Will you draw your line in the sand? Draw the line that says, "On this day, at this time, with this person, based on this Scripture, I choose freedom. I choose life." Don't hesitate. Silly as it may sound, it will stop the leak causing the mess.

The line in the sand will stop the drip in your head.

Your line in the sand is part of the process of walking in continued freedom. Your line in the sand stops the leak. Your line in the sand is your certainty. Put it on paper. Carry that piece of paper in your wallet, in your purse, or in your car. Keep it beside your bed. Put in on your refrigerator. Stick it to your bathroom mirror. Learn it. Rehearse it. Speak it. Shout it. Sing it. It's your line in the sand that reminds you that you are free.

MY LINE IN THE SAND

_____

Date

_____

Time

_____

Place

_____

Person

_____

Scripture

_____

Outcome

Now get busy living past the moment. Let nothing rob you again. Let no feeling or emotion steal your moment. Let no amount of fear, anxiety, guilt, torment, anger, jealousy, lust, hurt, disappointment, abuse, or frustration hijack the moment when your hope was regained. Don't run backward. Run forward. You are free. Hope has risen. Never again be lazy about your process of freedom. It may take some work, but it's worth every bit of effort you will put forth. When you define your line in the sand, the potential of your being better is **100 percent guaranteed**. You will grow stronger; it will get better. I guarantee it.

Never forget your moment. Rehearse it. It's the catalyst for your faith. It's how you will walk free. It's how you will find the freedom you have so longed to enjoy. Now that your moment is defined, it is time to move into learning to live beyond the moment. Now that your line in the sand is drawn, we can start making some progress. Every day is a day further away from your mess. Hint: You should already be rehearsing your line in the sand.

Your line in the sand is the certainty of your freedom.

Chapter 12 Reality Check

1. Can you identify any out-of-control emotion that you are tolerating? If it's detrimental to you, then why do you tolerate it?

2. How does this statement play into your freedom: "The mess stops here and now, regardless of how I feel"?

3. Explain this phrase: "Your line in the sand stops the drip in your head."

4. Have you written your line in the sand? Keep rehearsing it. Memorize it.

5. Is there anything holding you back from stating, "The mess stops here and now"?

6. Why is it often a struggle to ask others to help us when we are in a mess?

7. Who is the person who will help hold you to your line in the sand?

8. How can your line in the sand be "the certainty of your freedom"?

9. Are you willing to toe your line in the sand without making excuses? What do you think will be your biggest excuse—should an excuse arise?

10. Is there a thought now that discourages you from believing your line in the sand will work? What is that thought? What will you do to take responsibility for that thought?

CHAPTER 13

Are You Willing to Risk It?

"Freedom always requires a degree of risk."

RISK—it confronts your insecurities. RISK—it exposes your hidden fears. RISK—it challenges your real beliefs. RISK—it burns your security blankets. RISK—without it, you get nowhere in life. Without risk, you will find yourself tethered to a web of mediocrity. Do you know one reason many never find freedom? Do you know why people rarely press toward a better life? Do you know why many, despite their passion, will struggle to live out long-term freedom and realize their dreams? RISK! It's just too risky to move forward. Whether we like it or not, change for the better always requires a degree of risk. Your comfort zone will be at risk. Your familiar habits will be at risk. Your securities will be at risk. Risk is risky, to be sure.

Big dreams require big risks.

I've noticed this principle in my own life. Because of the risks required for pursing my plan A and moving toward a better life, I found myself always taking the easy road. In high school, I took the classes that seemed least demanding. In college, I went the easy route. It was simple—I had **big dreams**, but the path I chose never equated to the dreams I had. I wanted to change lives. I wanted to see the world impacted via my own life. Oh, how easy it was to dream big. But mark this quote down in your memory banks: "Big dreams require big risks." If you are going to DREAM BIG, then you must be willing to RISK BIG.

Better is never possible without risk. *Mediocre* requires nothing. *Better* requires risk. *Mediocre* feeds off familiarity. You will never get better if you are not willing to risk familiarity. Did you know that it's impossible to even discuss Christianity without bumping head-on into the issue of risk? It's all over the Bible, story after story. Ponder Noah, who's the topic of Genesis 6. Minding his own business, quietly raising his family, God shows up to introduce a profound challenge to him. It's a challenge so risky it will forever influence the world to come. Can you imagine the conversations in his house the day Noah came home from speaking with God? "Um, honey, I have to build a boat. I was outside tending to the farm, and God came down from heaven and told me to build a boat because He is going to destroy every creature and put an end to the whole earth." Oh, don't you know that the husband-wife conversation must have heated up after that opening monologue.

My imagination lends me to believe it went something like this.

MRS. NOAH: A BOAT? A boat to save the world, and there's not even a cloud in sight? Some voice came out of the sky and told you to build a boat? How do you plan on finding time to build a boat? Who's going to help you? Me? I've got to tend to these kids of yours and keep the house up and food cooked, and now what? You want me to go out and man the farm while you go traipsing off through the woods to build you a boat? A boat? Wonder why God didn't tell you to build me a house? Roof is leaking, dirt's all on the floor, and you have some newfound inspiration to spend all your energy building a boat?

NOAH: Well, that's what He asked me to do. He said He was going to destroy the earth, and I was supposed to build this boat.
MRS. NOAH: And how do you suppose you are going to afford to build this boat?
NOAH: Well, He told me I was to build it out of GOPHER WOOD.
MRS. NOAH: GOPHER WOOD?

NOAH: Yep.

MRS. NOAH: Well, it's a good thing He told you to GOPHER wood 'cause I ain't got time to go for wood!

NOAH: Hmm, just one final thing. The boat has to be four hundred and fifty feet long, forty-five feet high, and seventy-five feet wide.

MRS. NOAH: And you're gonna put this boat where? In our front yard? You best get busy 'cause we got the boys' birthdays coming up next month.

NOAH: Oh, I meant to tell you. It's going to take more than one hundred years to build it. So…

Are you willing to risk whatever it takes to find your freedom?

Do you get the point by now? How ludicrous the task of building that boat must have seemed to Noah and his family. Noah had to drop everything he knew in order to spend the next one hundred years of his life on one crazy request. "BUILD GOD A BOAT!" It would be a risk for sure. First, Noah would risk the fact that if he built the boat, his family might not join him on the boat. What if his wife left him? What if his boys thought he was off his rocker? Would his **family** simply follow suit behind his *illogical obedience*? It was Noah's first big risk.

Next, he had to risk letting go of his own *dreams*. I'm sure Noah didn't wake up that day with the lifelong dream of being a boatbuilder. He was a farmer. He worked the land, not the sea. However, taking on the task of becoming a boatbuilder would put his dreams at risk. He risked his farm and his **dreams** to build God's boat.

To complete the task, Noah had to risk his own **happiness**. Can you imagine one hundred years spent doing the same thing? Day in and day out, one hundred years of the same ol' mundane tree hunting, tree cutting, tree stacking, and boatbuilding routine must have been disheartening. No more carefree days of his casual grape-growing passion. His hands were now bloodied and calloused and filled with splinters rather than stained with grapes. His back was now sore from hoisting logs forty-five feet into the air. And it's almost a given that the farm was suffering and in dire need of tending.

Next, Noah had to risk his **reputation**. What would the community think of his newfound endeavor? Wonder how many friends he thought he'd lose? Obviously, he lost them all, for the Bible gives us no record of any relative, neighbor, or friend lending a helping hand. Everyone thought him to be the town lunatic. Even knowing this, he risked it.

Finally, he had to risk **failing God**. What if on the day of the flood the boat sprung a leak? What if it didn't float? What if the weight ratio to water displacement was miscalculated and the boat sank? What if Noah's boat failed and he destroyed all remaining earth creatures due to his lack of training and inability to pilot the vessel? What if they ran out of food? What if the animals ate one another? What if his wife was allergic to big cats? What if they got sick and died? All of the above are valid questions. Why risk it? No, thank you. But NOAH? He was willing to risk it.

Better is never possible without risk.

Noah risked his family. He risked his dreams. He risked his happiness. He risked his reputation. He risked failing God. Yes. He risked it **all**. As a result, you and I are here today, alive and well, because some man dared to risk it all to follow God. A man you never met before took a huge risk so your life could continue on this planet. As a matter of fact, perhaps we should all pause and be thankful that Noah took such risk so that all humanity could enjoy the reward. Noah's willingness to get calluses and splinters brought great reward to us all.

In that thought alone lies a deep truth. In Noah's willingness to accept the risks, you are now able to enjoy the reward. The REWARD demanded the RISK. This is the culprit behind most failure. The reward never seems worth the risk. The **reward** is the dream, the fantasy, and the desires long awaited. But if the reward doesn't hold more value than the risk, you will never take the risk. Believe me, when people see the potential of reward, they will take the risk. It's the motivating force behind gambling.

So I ask you, is the potential of finding your freedom worth the risk? Is the potential of ending your mess worth the risk? Are you willing to risk familiar habits? Are you willing to risk being uncomfortable? Are you willing to risk happiness? Are you willing to risk reputation? Are you willing to risk friends? Are you willing to risk family? Are you willing to risk failure? Are you really willing to risk anything it takes for you to have a better life? If you want to have your best life ever and reap the greatest of rewards for you, your family, and your future, then you must ask yourself the hard question: are you willing to risk all the old, familiar, and comfortable ways to experience the new and better way?

REWARD = RISK

Years ago, my dad made a simple statement to me that changed how I viewed my faith. He said, "Mark, you will never step out in faith if you are not willing to fail." To walk by faith is a risk. Self always seeks comfort and security. Faith always moves you past comfort and security to take you into the realm of trusting God. I pose this question to you: "Are you willing to risk trusting God to find your rest?"

The decision you must make requires your willingness to risk whatever it takes to break free of any emotions hindering you from living a great life. Depression, loneliness, hurt, bitterness, and mistrust may be your normal way of living. To break from your normal way of living may take some risk. Don't be afraid to take that risk. Change is risky. But if you are in a mess, change is what you so desperately need.

Don't succumb to some old habit because the threats of change are too risky.

The fear attached to the decision to "risk it" is why most people continue in a cycle of tolerance. Tolerance is easy, while change feels hard—too hard. The threat of parting with your comfortable habits is a risk you may feel you cannot take. It is possible to have become so comfortable with how things are that it's hard to view life any other way. Let's look at a passage of Scripture in the gospel of John that I think will shed some insight into taking a risk to find freedom. It's the story of a fellow who spent thirty-eight years in a mess and seemingly had no way of escape.

Afterward Jesus returned to Jerusalem for one of the Jewish holy days.
2 Inside the city, near the Sheep Gate, was the pool of Bethesda, with
five covered porches. 3 Crowds of sick people—blind, lame, or para-
lyzed—lay on the porches. 5 One of the men lying there had been sick
for thirty-eight years. 6 When Jesus saw him and knew he had been
ill for a long time, he asked him, **"Would you like to get well?"**
JOHN 5:1–6 (NLT)

Did you notice the risk this man has to confront to find freedom? This
risk lies within a question: **"Would you like to get well?"** The answer to
that question should be an obvious YES! However, let's look at the man's
response.

"I can't, sir," the sick man said, "for I have no one to put me into the pool
when the water bubbles up. Someone else always gets there ahead of me."
JOHN 5:7 (NLT)

This verse reveals a man whose life suffers from the hopelessness of
ever being better. Notice all the intricacies of the story. The years have
brought the invalid to a place where his life is **stuck**. His emotions, his
potential, and his desires are stuck. Yet Jesus steps into the scenario to offer a way out.

Do you want to be made well?

Do you? Maybe one reason you are where you are is that your actions and
emotional habits outweigh your desires. Maybe you *don't* want to be better.
Obviously, the lame man wanted to get well. You would think the answer is so
obvious that Jesus wouldn't even have to ask him that question. I think Jesus is
giving us insight into the human psyche by posing the question, "Would you
like to be made well?" God has the ability to make us better, but He knows if
we don't risk living better, we will revert to our same old patterns.

Let's read further into our friend's story, just a few verses later after Jesus
has healed the man.

14 But afterward Jesus found him in the Temple and told him, "Now you are well; so stop sinning, or something even worse may happen to you." 15 Then the man went and told the Jewish leaders that it was Jesus who had healed him. 16 So the Jewish leaders began harassing Jesus for breaking the Sabbath rules.
JOHN 5:14–16 (NLT)

Wow! Did you see what happened there? Just like our friend in the Scripture, God wants you changed into a radically different person. It is no problem for God to bring your freedom to you. Look at verse fourteen where Jesus says, "so stop sinning." In other words, Jesus says, "You are healed. Now change the habits that will hinder the freedom you've found."

Then Jesus goes a step further by saying, "or something even worse may happen to you." Amazing! That is a harsh reality. Are you willing to open yourself to this truth? Jesus is willing, Jesus can, and Jesus wants to heal you. However, He requires that *you* be part of your ongoing freedom. He will get you through it all by grace. Your freedom is His work. Your old ways can be your undoing.

Your continued freedom lies in your willingness to risk letting go of your old habits.

How many times has God intervened in your mess? How many times have you, in turn, made the mess worse? I have a saying when I counsel someone who faces this predicament. I always say, "Don't make another mess out of the mess God has already cleaned up." Don't be lulled into thinking that your freedom is all on God's shoulders. Don't believe the lie that He will "do it all," and you will simply sail on the winds of victory. Jesus can bring you certain freedom from your mess, but you must risk letting go of the habits that are causing your mess.

Yes, initial deliverance resides solely in the grace and ability of God. Jesus is going to offer you a free and clear way out of anything. It's free! There is nothing you can do to earn His initial help and deliverance. However, if you do not replace your old habits, stop your old ways of thinking, and renew your mind to the "new norm," you will digress into the same bondage from which you were freed.

Familiarity is the enemy of risk.

My favorite period of American history is the era of the civil rights movement. It was a period flawed and marked by familiarity and tolerance. What had been tolerated for centuries, accepted for decades, and recognized for years was about to come to blows with one simple decision. It would be a decision spurred by a single lady who decided that risk was greater than the tolerance. On December 1, 1955, in Montgomery, Alabama, Rosa Parks, age forty-two, refused to obey bus driver James Blake's order to give up her seat to make room for a white passenger. The future was about to be written, not by the pen of tolerance but by the hand of risk.

God bless Rosa Parks. She was willing to break with the tolerable and risk the familiar in order for her destiny to be resolved to its fullest potential. She could have ridden the bus on that December afternoon like every other day, but she didn't. She decided to leave the familiarity of the mess caused by racial divide and took a huge risk. Her individual choice would catapult countless others toward freedom—REWARD—because she was willing to break the cycle—RISK. REWARD = RISK. GLORY TO JESUS! She was willing to live beyond the moment. She was willing to risk everything in the moment so she could enjoy the reward of freedom she so deserved. She woke up with a plan in mind and she broke free.

Perhaps Ms. Parks' plan was not written on paper. Perhaps her plan was not distinctively and specifically premeditated. But she had fixed a plan, nonetheless. It was a plan in her heart that stated, "Tolerance, mediocrity, and fear are no longer going to define my future." On that bus, she took her first step toward freedom. Her plan put into action was simple. It was as simple as refusing to give up a seat. But it was her decision to risk it all that catapulted an entire nation forward.

I pray you are no longer willing to ignore or tolerate emotional habits in your life. I pray you wake up from the nightmare that emotional habits create and move into the reality of freedom and peace beyond measure. I pray you choose to make a decision to **leave the familiarity** of your issue and press toward the unknown realm of freedom that has eluded you for years. I pray you get tired of the mediocrity. I pray you hate the familiarity of your mess. I pray that you be willing to end any behavior that thwarts your best life ever. And I pray you RISK whatever it takes to reap a great REWARD.

Will you risk where you are for where you want to be?

Ask yourself is getting better worth risking your level of comfort and security? If you are not willing to embrace risk, then getting better is not possible. If you can't risk where you *are* for where you want to *be*, then you will always regress—regardless of how much God helps you. Sadly, you will always fall short.

So, be honest with yourself. Sit down, take a moment and answer these questions. Is your freedom worth the risk? Are you willing to walk out the freedom God will give you? Will you rise to the challenge? Will you, like Noah, be willing to risk it all? Will you, like the lame man, be willing to take up your bed and walk? Decide now to **accept the challenge**. Readjust your thoughts to secure sure and certain freedom, and then be willing to take the risk. Make the decision to have a funeral for the old you and risk unveiling the new. I promise you, you will never regret it.

Risk your familiar. Find your freedom.

Chapter 13 Reality Check

1. Define the phrase "REWARD = RISK."

2. What REWARD are you seeking on the other side of your mess? If you can't clearly define your reward, it's hard to validate the risk.

3. Are you more REWARD focused or REALITY focused? (Reward focused is believing there is change for the better that's ahead for you. Reality focused is simply succumbing to the concept of "it is what it is.")

4. If the reward (the dream you so desire to achieve) doesn't outweigh the risk (what you will have to give up or change), you will never experience a better life. Are you truly willing to risk whatever it takes?

5. Make a list of things you are going to have to risk to be better.

6. Do you want to be well? If you answered "yes," are you willing to break from all the old habits? Are you willing to risk your "old normal" for a "new normal"? List some old habits you need to end.

7. How does this sentence apply to you—"Getting better is going to require risk"?

8. Why is risk a scary thing?

9. How will a risk for better affect your security, your comfort, your friends, and your family?

10. Are you afraid of failure? Explain.

CHAPTER 14

Want a Life? Get a Plan!

"What if you're asking God for a miracle, but He's asking you to break a habit?"

L iving a life of long-term continued freedom is certainly possible. You don't have to live fearful of losing the freedom Jesus promises you. Your continual freedom is grounded in your working out what God has worked within. I would like to teach you the skills to make sure that your freedom will be long lasting. Once you gain the skills to walk out your process of freedom, not only will you get better, but you will also remain better. I guarantee it. How is it possible for me to guarantee you will get better when I don't know the battle you are facing? My assumptive guarantee may seem rather arrogant at first.

Let me put it this way, "The potential for you to get better is a 100 percent guarantee." Wherever you are at this moment—home, office, hotel room, or even in a closet—you have within you the potential to become better. I want you to see that there is no magical formula for deliverance and freedom. All you require is some good old-fashioned chutzpah for the journey.

Lazy never wins the battle.

You cannot get better if you are lazy about getting better. You won't make progress by wishing it to happen. You make progress by working on it. We've had thousands of years as humans to deal with our messes. Yet each generation, each culture, each day, each person has proven that our messes are not healed by the passing of time alone. Have you not yet noticed that laziness doesn't work? Ignoring your problem doesn't make it disappear. Tolerance doesn't make it any less frustrating. Many people say they are "hopeful." They say they trust God. They may even say they are "waiting on God to fix their mess." But in reality, they are simply lazy about being better. It may sound harsh, but like my guarantee, it's 100 percent true.

Passion without a plan is like a dream you never wake up from.

Have you found yourself stuck in this cycle? One week, you are passionately pursuing your dream. The next week, you regress. Then you try again for a week or two until you feel too tired. And the saga continues. It's haphazard effort at best. There is no plan. There is no well-thought-out process of how to reach your dream. It's just wishing for a dream. It's passion but with no real plan. You have become what I call haphazardly lazy.

Haphazard laziness causes you to remain busily frustrated with no obvious plan of action. You're hoping, wishing, crossing fingers, and waiting intently for some miraculous moment to arrive and whisk you out of your mess, but nothing is happening. You make decisions but don't fight to stick to them. Rather than living with a goal in mind, you live with the problem in mind. However, when you want to walk in continual freedom, it is going to take a well-laid-out **plan of action** to make certain you don't regress to your emotionally weak ways.

Sadly, I have found that most people never make a plan to get out of their mess. They want some wind to blow, some prayer to be prayed, or for God to do some instant miracle so the mess will all magically go away. However, most emotional dysfunction doesn't magically disappear after a prayer or a confession of Scripture. Why? Freedom isn't always immediate when the answer is found in a habit that must be broken rather than in a miracle that needs to be performed.

What if your freedom is connected to a habit that needs to be broken?

I cannot tell you how many times after I'd prayed or quoted Scripture I would find myself falling back into the same old patterns of thinking. I went to the altar countless times hoping for some quick, miraculous relief only to find myself no different afterward. I came to the conclusion that there must be **something more** I needed to do. I wanted a miracle; God wanted to break a habit. I wanted instantaneous results; God wanted continual obedience.

Ponder this: what if you're asking God for a great miracle, but He's asking you to break a bad habit? To break bad habits, you need good plans. You cannot make wishes and hope things will change. You must be willing to get a plan of action. You must shake yourself. Understand this: if you want to see mediocre vanish, if you want to live happy and satisfied, if you desire to live fulfilled and contented, then you are going to have to devise a **plan of attack**. You can't just remain lazy, hoping some magical moment is going to arrive to whisk you into a better life.

I have four daughters. That means somewhere in my future, I will have provided four weddings. So far, one wedding is down and there are three more to go. I cannot even fathom trying to pull off these events with no plan. I could not imagine spending the required energy, passion, and money for that day, that hour, with no plan in mind. No, sir. In fact, society as a whole rarely wings a wedding. We hire coordinators, photographers, musicians, and clergy to pull off the special day. We arrange and plan the minute details down to seating charts and marking where the wedding party is supposed to stand. Music is orchestrated, vows are written, dresses are hemmed, flowers are arranged, and even the candid photography is planned. The wedding day is a well-coordinated effort, mapped out for one thing—SUCCESS. Every bride longs for everything to proceed flawlessly!

But there is **a kink** in this wheel. After the wedding is complete, the new bride and groom run off for some wonderfully intimate alone time. However, as soon as they arrive home, there is **no instruction manual** showing them how to live. There is no plan. There is no coordinator. There is no one to assist them in postwedding life. They have no plan on how to stay happily married. They are merely hoping that their emotions can keep them committed and in love. Yet, what is the often-pending result? All of the habits that were put on hold during the well-planned ceremony resurface during those ill-planned posthoneymoon years to come. And because of the not-yet-mapped-out future together, old habits always ensue and can easily disintegrate any residue of love that remains.

A great plan will guarantee a great future.

Let me share with you a true story that will hopefully inspire you to devise a plan of success. It's a story about the power of a plan. It's a miracle that was birthed out of a plan to create new habits. Years ago, I stood on the sands of a Savannah beach one night to unite two dear friends in marriage. Both of them had come from previous broken marriages, and I knew that the likelihood of success, statistically, was very miniscule. They were starting their new marriage with extreme odds stacked against them. At the time of their union, neither person was really serving God, but they were intent on starting a new life together in hopes that their love would prevail.

You can guess the end result. As statistics would predict, two years later, the marriage was at an end. The new love was soon conquered by old emotional habits. The players had changed, but the habits remained the same. Habits they had developed through years of hurt, pain, disappointment, and poor decisions left little hope for a long-term happy couple. It was a marriage built on love and laziness. It was a marriage brought together by love and emotion but brought to an end by lack of planning.

I received the news in a dreaded phone call one afternoon while sitting in my office. "Mark, the marriage is over. She left me and has filed for divorce." I was so sad. I hated to see this outcome. Yet I knew in my heart there was still hope. I knew God could bring a miracle out of their marital mess if given the opportunity. After our conversation, I immediately texted his wife to encourage her toward reconciliation, but I did not get the response I had hoped for. "It's over," she replied. "Don't even try to get us back together. I made a commitment to myself years ago that I would never tolerate being miserable again." So I obliged. I simply offered a prayer and stated that I believed God could give her hope. It seemed all was lost. Hopelessness was rampant, and old habits were dictating present realities. However, I refused to lay down hope for this couple. So I began to pray for a plan.

Victory! One week away from the divorce being final, the wife decided to withdraw the divorce proceedings. I was elated when I got the call. So we all got together and decided to get a plan for **success**. First, they physically tore up the divorce proceedings. Then they wrote out their plan for success. They wrote how they would break with old habits, handle disagreements, discipline children, and learn to fight for their future without reverting to old habits. They confronted fears, talked about weaknesses, and identified problem areas.

They wrote every decision for success. They created a manual for their success. They built a box so they could fill it with all the reasons why they were thankful for each other. They **confronted** their habits. They regained hope. They decided to trust. They **readjusted** their thinking. They took a risk. By doing so, they broke the cycle of failure by devising and working a plan.

The end result was unexpected, unprecedented, undeniable SUCCESS. They conquered a hopeless situation with a simple decision to stop living by emotions alone and start living by a plan. They broke from the old dysfunctional habits and took a risk to plan out the new life they desired. They were willing to live past the moment and live out the plan. They pursued **a great future** because they entered into a process of living by a plan rather than responding to an emotion. They dealt a final deathblow to haphazard laziness. Today, they are living their decisions, not reaping their reactions. Now they are a success story, not a statistical nightmare.

Your story can be a success story rather than a nightmare.

The moral of the story? They were willing to risk it. They were willing to get a plan. Their miracle didn't come at an altar during a church service. Their miracle came after a prayer that produced a plan. And the simple truth, if the plan is pursued and the decisions are kept, then their freedom and success will be continual. However, if the plan is laid aside, hope is lost, and the shift moves back to emotional fortitude alone with failure as the consequence. Even the best-laid plan will fail when you do not live the plan.

If you are going to walk out your continual freedom, you must be willing to pray for a plan. No matter how hard others try to help, you cannot overcome without a plan. If you have no plan, then your emotions will always dictate your response. Your result will always be one riddled by failure. Planning takes effort, willingness, energy, and confrontation. Planning makes you face the fact that you really do need a plan.

Are you willing to admit you can't be lazy about your life any longer? Remember, lazy never wins the battle. Are you ready to confront the issue? Confrontation isn't as scary when you have a plan in place. Many fail at success because they cannot endure the shaky, unstable bumps in the journey. Why? They navigate without a plan. It's always easier to revert to the comfort of your old ways when you have no clear plan of action to follow.

Stop praying your problem and start praying your plan.

Therein lies the diagnosis of most failures. They start with passion but fail at planning. If you desire to live a satisfied, mess-free life, you must devise a plan. You must be willing to stop being lazy and get busy writing out your plan. Don't simply make a decision in your head. Take some time. Write your vision down. Write down your **plan**. You WILL become what you write. You don't have to succumb to being what your emotions or your situations dictate. You are your vision. Once you get a plan, you can stop praying your problem and start praying your plan.

So sharpen your pencil, and let's build a plan together. Breaking from the deathblow of laziness starts by getting a plan and then deciding to work your plan despite the risk. Without a plan, the mess in your head will always win. If you want to stave off future messes, put your pencil to paper and begin writing. Write down **every detail** of what you know you can do to take steps in the right direction. Write a plan for how you will respond to pressure. Write a plan for handling frustration the next time it arises. Write a plan for how you will confront your fear. Write a plan for your marriage. Write a plan for better health. Write a plan for a better life. Write a plan that guides your emotions when they falter.

Bottom line: start writing down your plan of action. Live your plan. If you do so, you will soon be well on your way to living in complete and total freedom. If you write your plan, if you read it daily, and if you decide to live your plan, you will conquer your mess and fulfill the dreams that have long been awaiting you.

It's better to live your plan than ruin your life.

Chapter 14 Reality Check

1. Do you have a written plan for the key areas of your life—spiritual, physical, financial, marriage, family, and profession? Is it written down on paper, not just in your head?

2. Explain your thoughts about this statement: "You are your vision. You are what you write down and define."

3. Why do you think there's so much more potential for success when you have a plan? How does this statement apply to you: "Passion without a plan is failure"?

4. Explain what is meant by this statement: "You have to stop praying your problem and start praying your plan." How will you apply it?

5. What are some consequences that arise when you live by emotion rather than by a plan?

6. What are the areas of your life where you are lazy? Are you lazy in your eating habits? Lazy in your thought life? Lazy in your marriage? Lazy in your health choices? Lazy in your parenting? Why have you let laziness rule these areas?

7. Are you more passionate or planned? What is the danger of having passion without a plan?

8. What if you are asking God for a miracle, but He's asking you to break a habit? What is a habit that may need breaking right now?

9. How can lingering habits hinder God's miracle power?

10. Are you willing to take the dream in your mind and make it a plan on paper? It's very difficult to reach your dreams when they stay in your head rather than written down in a plan. Write out a short five-step action plan for success. What is it going to take? What has to change? What thought patterns have to change?

CHAPTER 15

Stop Sabotaging Yourself

"God doesn't give you a do-over. He gives you mercy."

Through the years, I have noticed two things that sabotage most people from enjoying the long-term freedom they have found: their MEMORIES and their MOUTHS. Memories sabotage them because they can't stop thinking about their past: their failures, their hurts, and their disappointments. Their mouths sabotage them because they speak negativity and criticism all the time. Here's another truth: you'll never conquer the mess in your head if you keep sabotaging your success.

Your memories and your mouth can end your mess.

Memories and mouths—we've all got them and either one or both can get in the way of your freedom. You've got to stare into the future and silence all the haunting memories of your past that keep sabotaging your progress. And if you're really serious about long-term freedom, you've got to shut your mouth when it comes to speaking negatively about yourself. Concerning your messy past, you're not alone; we all have one. So deal with it. Don't pack a suitcase and carry it around with you. Buy a coffin and bury the mess.

Let me share with you a dream I had back in the early 1980s. It forever shifted the way I viewed dealing with my past.

I was standing in a living room preparing for a party. I was unsure whom or what the party was for, but I was cleaning and preparing to host a large number of people. As I finished cleaning, I noticed a person sitting in a recliner. I walked over to see who had come early. As I made my way, I realized that it was a good friend of mine sitting in the chair. He appeared to be asleep, so I shook him to wake him, hoping he would help me prepare for the party. He didn't move. I shook him again. No response. That's when I realized he was dead. In that instant, a knock came at the door. I didn't know what to do. I began to panic. I grabbed my friend, threw a large trash bag over him, and shoved him into the closet in hopes that no one would find him. Suddenly, the living room was filled with young teenagers. The house was buzzing with excitement, games, and fun. I found my way to the kitchen to make sure we had enough food for my guests. I was gone quite a while preparing snacks when I heard a group of teenagers laughing in the other room. I made my way back into the room and what I saw ter-rified me. They had discovered my dead friend, taken him out of the bag, sat him up in the recliner, and were feeding him Cheetos. (I know it may seem to be a comical situation now, but in the midst of my dream, it was a horror-filled moment for me.) My party guests were playing with him like he was a rag doll, moving his mouth, arms, and legs. They kept stuff-ing Cheetos into his mouth making jokes and laughing over his dead body. Suddenly, the atmosphere changed. My friend came back to life. He sat up in the chair and began to converse with all the teenagers. The whole group was in complete shock. The unexpected had happened. My dead friend was alive and well, eating Cheetos, and playing games. Suddenly and un-expectedly, he began attacking everyone in the room. Then I woke up.

That dream puzzled me for weeks. First, why was my friend dead? Was this a warning? How did he get into the house? How did the teens find him? How did he come back to life? Why was he attacking everybody? I pondered all these questions again and again. I would have let the dream go and decided it was a "bad pizza" dream, but I couldn't get the images out of my mind. So I determined to seek God to give me understanding and insight about my dream. Maybe I was missing something. It was after a day of long pondering when I heard God speak to my heart: "Closets are for clothes, not corpses." Ouch! I began to ponder that thought over and over. I came to realize that you should never try to bury your old habits and emotions in a closet. If you try to hide your emotions rather than deal with them, they will resurface on a rainy day and take you over.

Bury the mess of your past and it will no longer dominate you.

That's how the past sabotages you. You put a trash bag around it and throw it in a closet hoping no one else ever comes in contact with it. You don't **bury it**. And you don't really deal with it. But I promise you, if you don't bury the mess of your past, it will come back to haunt you when you least expect it. Actually, your past won't just haunt you; *it will do everything in its power to take you over and dominate you.* If you don't come to terms with your past mistakes and the messes they've made, you won't ever reach your true God-given potential. Don't fret your past. Don't regret your past. Don't hide your past. It's past. God can handle it. No matter how messy it looks, **God can** clean it up. Let God turn the mess of your past into the miracle message of your future. I promise you that your mess is not a shock to God. Jesus promised redemption of your mess when He made the statement, "Neither do I condemn you; go and sin no more" (John 8:11 [NLT]).

I have met many people who start making progress, but they soon reappear in my office with an inability to get over their past. The memories haunt them. The hurt is too great. The pain is too horrific. They often state, "I can't forget what happened. I can't get it out of my mind." Let me enlighten you to a great truth about your memories: God is not asking you to forget them; He's asking you to trust Him with them.

Never let your messy past sabotage your glorious future.

You are going to have to trust God with the memories. You must believe that God can make a miracle out of your mess. You must believe God can and will intervene in your past. You can't erase your past. You don't have the innate ability to forget it at will. You have to shift from the memories and the mess to the miracles and the rest. Obviously, memories replaying in your head will always be possible. So how are we to be free if we don't possess the ability to forget the past?

I was struggling with this very question. There was an issue of failure in my past, and I couldn't seem to shake that memory of it. I often thought, *How will I ever get past this issue because my memory of it constantly resurfaces and reminds me of the failure?* **If only** I could have another chance to repeat the past and perhaps come out a success. **If only** I had been smarter, wiser, or more aware. **If only** I could go back and have a do-over. **If only** I time-travel and resettle old accounts. But no such luck. I was stuck in the limitation of all humanity. As much as we'd like to, we can't go back to correct the horrors of our past. **If only...**

"If only" is not an option God gives to us. Do-overs and time travel are not options we've been afforded. It was clear to me that time travel was to be left for Hollywood movies. Movies make it look so easy and effortless. However, it's a mere fantasy that will lull you into a trap of constantly wishing you could go back and settle the past. Thankfully, I finally got the clue that mulling over my past was a waste of energy. So I began to ask God for wisdom on how to move past the memories causing my mess and live out my freedom beyond them.

I was certain about a lot of things. But how to get over my past failure wasn't one of them. I knew I was forgiven. I knew I was repentant. I had apologized to the best of my human ability. I prayed nightly for restoration of hurts I had caused and friends I lost. I quoted Scripture. I cried. I rehearsed it. I cursed it. I tried even ignoring it. Yet, I wasn't able to shake free of the past and the memories associated with it. Then God spoke to my heart about how I was sabotaging my own freedom, and I was enlightened by one simple truth. It came through reading a Scripture. It was in the book of Lamentations.

> **22** *The faithful love of the Lord never ends!*
> *His mercies never cease.* **23** *Great is his faithfulness;*
> *his mercies begin afresh each morning.*
> LAMENTATIONS 3:22–23 (NLT)

It became clear to me why God would never offer us humans a do-over. We don't get a do-over; we get MERCY. We want God to give us a do-over, and God wants to give us His mercy. What a difference that makes.

You don't get a do-over; you get mercy.

If you could correct the mistakes of your own past, you would certainly feel better about yourself. However, mercy allows God to move you **forward** and establish your **future**; therefore, you certainly feel better about God. A do-over lets you feel better about yourself. Asking for mercy lets you feel better about God. A do-over would be past oriented and would confine you to walk in circles again and again. Mercy is future oriented and thrusts you toward walking in your destiny. A do-over allows you to "redeem yourself." Mercy allows God to "**redeem you.**" If God gave any of us a chance to go back and correct our past, then we would never truly know what it means to trust His redeeming power.

The worst day of your life can become the first day of your testimony.

You have to say to your past, "God redeemed you and you will no longer dictate my tomorrows!" No matter how shameful you feel, how horrible you appear, how desperate you've become, or how long you've tolerated your circumstances, today you can make one final decision to "let God's mercy redeem your mess." Stop sweating yesterday. Stop trying to forget it. If you could forget it, you wouldn't need mercy. Let mercy redeem your past.

The fact that you need mercy is a great thing. It's not a tragedy. It's a testimony. The most horrible mess you've made can become the greatest miracle you've ever experienced. You've waited for your past to walk in the room and haunt you. Well, start expecting God to walk in the room. Start expecting His Divine intervention. His glory, His weight, His power, and His mercy will overshadow your mess; He will **totally redeem** your mess if you just **let go** and trust Him with it.

You are not called to forget; you are called to remember.

So don't fret over your past anymore. Cease the effort and energy to avoid and forget your past. You're not called to forget. You are called to remember. Make certain that what you remember is not the mess you've made but the mercy He offers. Stand up and dust yourself off. You're not the only one who's been depressed, disappointed, hurt, disillusioned, shipwrecked, broke, sick, isolated, afraid, jealous, miserable, tired, molested, raped, abandoned, frustrated, or defeated. Welcome to humanity. Welcome to the club. We all have terrible messes we face. We all wish for a do-over. We all need mercy. I can tell you that those who bemoan the mess are miserable. However, those who celebrate His mercy are joyful.

So now you have some decisions facing you. Sabotage or celebrate? Do-over or mercy? Tragedy or testimony? It's up to you. God is waiting patiently on your choice. Truthfully, humanity is waiting on your decision. All of heaven is waiting. Time isn't going to heal the mess in your head. It's your decisions that are going to clean up the mess. It's time to decide to move forward and move beyond the memory by celebrating the mercy. I say **decide** to celebrate. Decide for mercy. Decide for testimony.

Last, I would be remiss if I let you move toward freedom without reminding you of one thing: your mouth determines your mess or your miracle. So I write to you this admonition: Enough is enough! Shut your mouth! If you can't say something positive, hush! The Bible says even a fool is thought wise if he keeps his mouth shut. So blow out the candles. Turn out the lights. Throw out the trash. Eat the last piece of cake.

Your pity party needs to end now.

That's as clear as I can make it. The party's over. Your memories can either rehearse your mess or release God's potential. Your mouth can either curse your past or bless your future. So before you cry over spilled milk or open your mouth to complain about your mess, answer one last question:

Will you bemoan your mess or celebrate His mercy?

I urge you to never again bemoan your mess. Use your mouth and your memories to celebrate God's wonderful mercy offered to you. Build a bridge to His mercy via your mouth. Exchange the memories of your mess for the message of your testimony. The past that has haunted you and the emotions that have created the mess no longer need to rule your life. Mercy rules your life. Don't sabotage your future potential with your memories or your mouth. Your past doesn't predict your future. Your mess doesn't reflect your potential. The party's over.

The mess of your past can be the message of God's mercy.

Chapter 15 Reality Check

1. Does your mouth line up with your desires?

2. Explain the phrase, "You can't move forward if you don't get a handle on your memories and your mouth."

3. Take a moment and write down one thing about your past that concerns you. Now claim mercy over it. Let the mess you are holding in your hand be the miracle God holds in His hand. Don't be ashamed of your past. Let it go.

4. Explain this statement: "Your mess can be the beginning of His miracle."

5. Is there a specific memory that keeps recurring that sabotages you? What is it?

6. How does this apply to your present situation: "You don't get a do-over; you get mercy"?

7. How does this make you feel: "The worst day of your life can be the first day of your testimony"?

8. One way to move forward is to rehearse your good memories on a daily basis. Often, the memories connected to your mess like to shout the loudest. Make a list of ten good memories that you are thankful for. Each time you feel yourself slipping toward the memories connected to your mess, verbally speak out your good memories and how you are thankful for them.

9. If God promises us mercy, why do we connect so much shame to our messy past?

10. Every time a memory of your mess resurfaces, don't let discouragement sink in. Think about that memory. Don't deny it or try to bury it. Think about it. Then pray this out loud:

> *"I will no longer let shame govern my messy past. The mess of my past is the message of His miracle. My mess isn't about my failure. My mess is about God's mercy. I choose mercy."*

CHAPTER 16

Make War, Not Love

"Your emotional mess requires a battleground, not a bakery shop."

If you want continued freedom, you must make war with your negative emotions, not love. You can't continue a love affair with your emotions and expect any long-term success. So many times, we are in involved in such a deep love relationship with our emotions that learning to live any other way becomes seemingly impossible. We have shacked up with the anger, rage, jealously, pain, disappointment, and hurt for so long that those emotions have become the **objects of our affection**. The anger becomes my mistress. The fear becomes my soul mate. The anxiety becomes my partner. You must stop this love affair with your emotions.

Declare war on the mess in your head.

If you want freedom, cease coddling fantasy and get busy changing reality. You can't continue in negativity, criticism, regret, depression, and disappointment if you want to live in complete, lasting freedom. You are going to have to fight. You are going to have to die to the old and begin to live for the new. You are going to have to bury the emotions that used to be your friends so they don't come back to haunt you. Like any good soldier, you have to learn how to fight the proper way.

One of the greatest hindrances to making war against emotions is the fact that giving up is easier than pressing forward. Many quit making progress toward freedom due to misunderstanding how to fight against their emotions in the correct way. When you don't learn how to fight the right way, you can never overcome. Your courage to press forward will slowly abate due to one simple deception we've all heard before: "It is easier to make love than war."

War of any kind is difficult, draining, and even oppressive. Warring against emotions on a consistent long-term basis is no exception. Have you ever noticed how wonderful emotions can make you feel? Even the worst of emotions can have a euphoric effect on your soul. The man addicted to anger finds his outbursts so deeply rooted in him that to be angry begins to satisfy some emotional drive. His anger becomes an aphrodisiac to his frustrations. The emotion that is killing him is the same emotion that is bringing much pleasure. *When you continually bed down with your emotions, you are dooming yourself to failure.* Otherwise, the emotions you're married to will become the emotions that rob you of all you hold dear.

Stop making love with your emotions and begin to battle your emotions.

A love affair with your emotional dysfunction presents grave problems. The emotions you love will produce the fruit you bear. The fruit you bear will be the things you nurture. You can't continue in a love affair with your past dysfunctional habits and expect to birth anything worthwhile in your future. No matter how much you pray, beg God, or seek His help, you cannot get good fruit from a bad root. To birth anything good in your future, you must begin to see your emotional mess as a battleground and not a bedroom.

Ponder this. We make appointments for the dentist, the doctor, the hairdresser, and countless other duties required in life. We put a sticker in the corner of our car's windshield to remind us when an oil change is due. We mark our calendars for our children's next gym meet and school function. However, we rarely schedule time to do something about our emotional health. Oh, you can bet we try to deal with our emotional mess through countless poor choices such as eating, drinking, sleeping, or taking pills to eradicate our mess. Astonishing how we will schedule in a myriad of things to make our lives as orderly and productive as possible, yet we merely "hope" that our unstable, emotional condition will dissolve without any planning or effort.

Therefore, it's time to declare war. When you make war on your emotions, you must make certain you fight right. You can't aimlessly think, *I'm going to make war on my emotions*, then paint your face like a Braveheart fan and yell "FREEDOM!" Mere passion alone won't cure the mess. You don't get free by living off emotional highs. You don't defeat your emotions by screaming, "I will never be depressed again!" You have to learn how to fight the right way. You get free by fighting to be free. So let's get some clarity on how to make war correctly. Remember in the previous chapter, "Closets are for clothes, not corpses." If you don't fight right, you'll have the wrong thing hiding out in your closet just waiting for a moment of resurrection.

It's easier to put our emotions in the closet rather than making war on them. First, you cannot fight if you are deceived. You have to war against your out-of-control emotions if you want freedom. I know firsthand that when emotional habits have been long-standing, they can feel like our security blankets. Coping mechanisms such as blaming everyone and everything else for my issues may pacify my conscience, but it brings me no closer to freedom. Your first step to fighting right is to make the determination that your bad emotional habits are just that—BAD. Sure, they may comfort you and ease some of your pain. But bad emotional habits will never get you to your destiny. Remember, it's impossible to get good fruit from a bad root. You have to put an end to your bad coping mechanisms.

Never let your emotions undermine your destiny.

Let's head back to the Bible and take a look at the life of Eve in chapter three of the book of Genesis. Emotions got her in a big ol' mess. She was living in a perfect world, created by a perfect God, in perfect union with her husband. She had no cares, no worries, no bills, no children, no pills, no ills, and no stress. Yet, she corrupted the entire human race with one small oversight.

Her emotions caught her in **a trap**. Her destiny was being lived out on a daily basis. Nevertheless, her emotions completely undermined and destroyed the destiny God had determined for her.

> *1 Now the serpent was more cunning than any beast of the field which the Lord God had made. And he said to the woman, "Has God indeed said, 'You shall not eat of every tree of the garden'?" 2 And the woman said to the serpent, "We may eat the fruit of the trees of the garden; 3 but of the fruit of the tree which is in the midst of the garden, God has said, 'You shall not eat it, nor shall you touch it, lest you die.'" 4 Then the serpent said to the woman, "You will not surely die. 5 For God knows that in the day you eat of it your eyes will be opened, and you will be like God, knowing good and evil." 6 So when the woman saw that the tree was good for food, that it was pleasant to the eyes, and a tree desirable to make one wise, she took of its fruit and ate. She also gave to her husband with her, and he ate. 7 Then the eyes of both of them were opened, and they knew that they were naked; and they sewed fig leaves together and made themselves coverings.*
> GENESIS 3:1–7 (NKJV)

Once Eve was caught in an emotional trap, she wasted no time playing the blame game. She blamed Satan for the deceit. But Satan didn't make Eve do anything. Satan had one plan. He had to get Eve to *want* to choose wrong. He knew he could not make her do anything she didn't want to do. So in a world of perfection, Eve forgot the one foundation for success. She forgot she could be **deceived**. *She trusted her emotions instead of truth and her choice was detrimental.* She allowed her emotions to govern her thoughts, and as a result, she was duped. Her decision to follow her emotional choice voided the freedom and perfection she once possessed.

This is one of the greatest truths about learning to fight right. Will you live your emotions, or will you live your faith? Which side are you going to fight on? Whichever side you choose, that's what you will become. You *are* your choices. Eve didn't fight right. Really, she really didn't fight at all. She simply did what she wanted to do. She didn't want to disobey and destroy humanity. She wanted to be like God. Her motive was pure *(I want to be like God)*, but her reasoning was deceived *(I want what I want)*. She wanted to be like God but on her own terms and in her own way.

Satan's greatest temptation: trust your emotions.

Eve's choice wasn't disobedience; it was passion and desire. But her longing—driven by out-of-control desire—could only be fulfilled through disobedience. To get her to disobey, Satan needed her to **choose** disobedience. Satan could not force her to disobey. He simply wooed her emotionally into choosing disobedience.

Satan had to tempt Eve to think she wasn't disobedient. He had to tempt her to think beyond God's command *(Don't eat from the tree)*. Satan needed Eve to think that her feelings could override God's commandment. He needed her to think that how she felt about God, the fruit, and herself was more important than the expressed commandment prescribed by God. In short, all Satan needed was for Eve to trust her **emotions**. Satan needed her to trust what she saw, how she felt, and what she desired more than she trusted God. And she did it. The deception was final and the destruction was complete. Satan wooed her into the deceit of trusting her emotions rather than trusting God.

When you war against your bad emotions, they will not woo you into a bad mess.

Is it not amazing that the first battle of human history was a battle over emotions? Eve longed for the wisdom. Eve desired the pleasure. And at the root of Eve's choice was an emotional battle that she lost. She pleased herself. She displeased God. Her emotions were wooed by the devil into a realm she dared not tread. Yet, tread she did. She jumped headlong into disastrous consequences all because her emotions trumped her God.

When you carry on a continual love affair with your out-of-control emotions, you are going to produce a life that's out of sync with God. A life that is out of sync with God will lead you to disobey God. Even if the emotion is not in direct disobedience to God's will, dysfunctional emotions will always move you into being out of God's will. As a result, all your choices will cause you to be out of sync with God's will.

Here is a critical component in making war against your emotions. Take note of this Scripture:

"And do not grieve the Holy Spirit of God, by whom you were sealed for the day of redemption."
EPHESIANS 4:30 (NKJV)

Your emotions can grieve the Holy Spirit. To grieve God simply means to bring Him sorrow. This is not some outward expression of God's sadness. But it is the expression of His internal state—sorrow. How can a human possibly make God sorrowful? When your emotions drive your life, you become out of sync with God—not in right relationship with Him. When you are not in right relationship with God, your life brings God sorrow. Why? Because He knows a life driven by emotions is doomed to suffer the consequences of disobedience.

You must also understand that your battle isn't against circumstances, feelings, or people. These battles aren't about some person, event, or feeling that defeats you. And just as it was in the beginning with Eve, you have an enemy working against you. It's your will versus God's will. The enemy's goal is to keep you out of sync with God. Satan wants you to live by emotional choices and decisions that will keep you from walking with God. If the enemy can keep you focused on your emotions, he knows that your life will cause God sorrow. The end result is guaranteed. You will live a disastrous life littered with disobedience, hurt, confusion, and pain. It's a no-win situation.

In every emotional battle, choose the will of God.

Satan's plan, his motive behind his designs, is to get you out of fellowship with God altogether so that a royal mess will be the course of your life. A Christian who is out of sync with God is destined for a life ruled by a mess. Why? Because when your life opposes God, you can never do the things you set out to do. Everything you try becomes a futile attempt for success. You'll never war against your emotions when you're in love with those emotions. And the mess can never be conquered when you won't go to war. This is why you must make war, not love, with your emotions—to be a life in sync with God and end the mess. Your negative, fleshly emotions can be conquered. You can win the war. You don't have to fear losing to negative emotions that keep you out of synch with the will of God. In every emotional battle, you can choose the will of God. Look at what the Apostle Paul writes in his letter to the Galatians:

> *17 The sinful nature wants to do evil, which is just the opposite of what the Spirit wants. And the Spirit gives us desires that are the opposite of what the sinful nature desires. These two forces are constantly fighting each other, so you are not free to carry out your good intentions. 18 But when you are directed by the Spirit, you are not under obligation to the law of Moses. 19 When you follow the desires of your sinful nature, the results are very clear: sexual immorality, impurity, lustful pleasures, 20 idolatry, sorcery, hostility, quarreling, jealousy, outbursts of anger, selfish ambition, dissension, division, 21 envy, drunkenness, wild parties, and other sins like these. Let me tell you again, as I have before, that anyone living that sort of life will not inherit the Kingdom of God. 22 But the Holy Spirit produces this kind of fruit in our lives: love, joy, peace, patience, kindness, goodness, faithfulness, 23 gentleness, and self-control. There is no law against these things! 24 Those who belong to Christ Jesus have nailed the passions and desires of their sinful nature to his cross and crucified them there. 25 Since we are living by the Spirit, let us follow the Spirit's leading in every part of our lives. 26 Let us not become conceited, or provoke one another, or be jealous of one another.*
> GALATIANS 5:17–26 (NLT)

Live by revelation not frustration.

Do you feel like you are failing in life? Haven't we all? I know I've felt like a failure many times. But despite my failure, I live with great hope. How so? The above verses were my medicine. I discovered freedom. I realized freedom by learning to let the Holy Spirit govern every realm of my emotional being. I lived by Holy Spirit revelation rather than succumbing to emotional frustration. The Holy Spirit became my way out. I saw it in the verses above. I came to realize the battle didn't have to be fought alone. I didn't have to fight by myself any longer. I had a guarantee for success. My guaranteed success was my willingness to be in step with the Holy Spirit. My success was following the Spirit's leading in every part of my life. My success was a merger of my emotions with His Divine power. This spiritual revelation was ending my emotional frustration.

It is simple: *self-control is a fruit of the Holy Spirit.* Did you catch that truth? Self-control is a fruit of the Spirit. You don't have to live feeling as if you cannot win the battle against your emotions. You may have been fighting with your emotions for years. But don't wave the white flag just yet. You can win. You will win. It may be a hard battle at first, but I know the Holy Spirit will prevail so you can begin to succeed in life. Make a commitment every morning to rehearse your thoughts. Make your mouth stop the negativity. Make your mind up to stop thinking like a failure. It's a time for strength, not weakness. It's time for war.

Get with your spouse, a friend, a pastor, or another believer in Christ and enlist someone else to stand with you in the battle. Meet weekly and battle together. When you decide to make war and enlist help, you are less likely to sabotage yourself in the process. Now get busy on the battlefront. Get busy stepping in line with God. Get busy about bringing God pleasure and achieving all He has called you to do. Get busy putting all of your energy and effort into making war against the out-of-control emotions that are leading you toward destruction. Determine that you are going to fight.

Your mess will be conquered when you go to war.

Chapter 16 Reality Check

1. What does this statement mean to you: "Don't let your emotions grieve the Holy Spirit"?

2. Explain how this impacts your situation: "You can choose to live your emotions or you can choose to live your faith."

3. Explain the phrase, "Your bad emotions can woo you into a bad mess."

4. "You can't make war against your emotions when you're in love with your emotions." Why?

5. What does making war on your emotions look like?

6. How can negative emotions get you out of sync with God's will?

7. Why would someone put effort into fixing and maintaining his or her vehicle yet neglect to provide the maintenance his or her emotions so desperately need?

8. Can you think of a time when you trusted your emotions over God's commandments? How did it turn out for you?

9. Have you made an appointment to talk with someone? Is your situation critical enough that you are willing to get help?

10. How would you explain this to someone: "Your journey determines your warfare. Your warfare determines your future"?

CHAPTER 17

Don't Use Your Energy To Quit

"This ain't your momma's sandbox."

Y ou may be thinking that you are too tired to make war with your emotions or to fight against anything. You may feel defeated and frustrated, thinking that the fight for freedom is a futile effort. However, take a moment to answer this critical question: "Do you want to spend your energy getting better or do you want to spend your energy meddling in the mess?"

**It takes more energy to tolerate your mess
than it takes to overcome it.**

Have you ever realized how much effort you have to put forth to continue tolerating your mess? I know it feels hard to overcome your mess because you have become comfortable with the pain and discomfort of tolerance. After years of counseling, I have heard many people say they don't have the will or energy to fight for a better life. By the time they sit inside the walls of my office, they are tired, defeated, and doubtful if the battle is even worth it.

It's easy to quit when you're spent.

The sad truth is, many never make an attempt at "better." They feel defeated, tired, disgusted, angry, hurt, frustrated, disappointed, and altogether spent. Why? Because all of the energy they have spent on their mess has been **distracted energy**. Mere existence and tolerance may seem effortless, but when it's built on a mess of emotions, it's a cesspool of **distracted energy**.

Let's define the phrase, "**distracted energy**." *Distracted energy* is energy spent analyzing, criticizing, and fantasizing over your problem. *Distracted energy* is energy spent maintaining the status quo. It is energy spent in mere existence. It's the energy wasted on excuses. When living with a mess in your head, great amounts of energy, effort, and time are spent on nothing. Behaviors such as analyzing, criticizing, and fantasizing keep you on a merry-go-round of progress that's headed nowhere. Going in circles may seem like you're seeing new things and experiencing different outcomes, but the mess always remains the same. A new vehicle, a new house, a new job, a new friend, a new hairdo, a new church, a new vacation spot, or even a new spouse won't create a new outcome. You can do all this and more and still ignore the fact that you are on a merry-go-round of dysfunction.

Maybe you feel spent? You do have energy to fight. It's in there. Maybe you feel so frustrated that any more effort seems futile. But if you are breathing, you have enough energy to begin the process. If you are reading this, then you have enough energy to enter the battle. If you are spent, it's not because the problem is too big or the devil is too powerful. It's because all of your energy has been distracted.

Success is guaranteed when you learn to fight right.

Your success is best achieved by putting the energy you have in the right place. Either you can fight by spending your efforts on *distracted energy* or you can learn to fight by focusing your effort on **attentive energy**. Attentive energy is effort spent on the things that really matter. It is the energy you focus toward achieving your goal. It's the energy you give to hope, kindness, love, forgiveness, patience, goodness, joy, and peace. It is the energy you use to stay in step with the Holy Spirit. *Attentive energy* is energy you spend keeping in sync with God. It's the energy you direct toward the sole purpose of one thing: **getting better**.

When you begin to put your efforts toward *attentive energy*, continual freedom becomes more certain. When you focus on *attentive energy*, the levels of discouragement, frustration, aggravation, and devastation begin to decline. *Attentive energy* escalates your potential of success to an exponential value. Your success is entirely determined by the focus of your energy. You may have heard this quote from my favorite movie, *The Shawshank Redemption*: "Get busy living, or get busy dying." Life or death—energy is needed for both.

Distracted energy is a merry-go-round. *Attentive energy* is a road map. *Distracted energy* is problem oriented. *Attentive energy* is solution oriented. *Distracted energy* is focused on the mess. *Attentive energy* formulates a plan of success. *Distracted energy* is mere feeling and emotion. *Attentive energy* is sweat and calluses. Are you getting the point? You do have enough energy. Otherwise, you wouldn't have been able to maintain your chaos and dysfunction. All of us have enough energy to overcome or to fail.

Spend your energy to overcome, not quit.

Statistically speaking, the energy you spend dealing with life is simply the result of how you noticed energy being spent as you were growing up. Was your childhood lived by watching *distracted energy*? Did you observe copious amounts of arguing, fighting, ignoring, criticizing, complaining, and abuse? All that was nothing more than a display of *distracted energy*. Perhaps you grew up with *attentive energy* being your model for life? Did your parents create a caring, patient, good, kind, thoughtful, and purposeful home?

In theory, what you witnessed as a child has a profound impact on how you make war today. Obviously, it becomes difficult to make war against your emotions when all you have seen are examples of *distracted energy*. Therefore, once you decide to make war with your emotions, you are going to have to enter the next phase of battle and determine which energy you will use. Will you war in a manner that's distracted or attentive?

It is not enough for you to make a dedicated determination to war against your emotions. That move doesn't equate long-term success. You must begin the battle with your energy **focused** on the right cause. Don't cower or act as if you can't muster the energy to overcome. You have enough energy to **win** this battle. You are blessed by God and have the opportunity to be alive. Now plan to make good use of that energy and attend to your success.

Stop expecting others to fight for you.

I want to share a story of how distracted energy can rob you of God's best for your life. It's found in 2 Samuel:11. Once again, we will glimpse into the story of King David and Bathsheba, the bathing beauty. This time, we will examine the portion of this tale that is the precursor to King David's demise. It will enlighten us to a downfall brought on by out-of-sync dysfunctional emotions.

> *1 In the spring of the year, when kings normally go out to war, David sent Joab and the Israelite army to fight the Ammonites. They destroyed the Ammonite army and laid siege to the city of Rabbah. However, David stayed behind in Jerusalem. 2 Late one afternoon, after his midday rest, David got out of bed and was walking on the roof of the palace. As he looked out over the city, he noticed a woman of unusual beauty taking a bath.*
> 2 SAMUEL 11:1–2 (NLT)

Hopefully, you can see what's taking place. We have a king, a bathing beauty, and a war. It occurred in springtime. There were soldiers willing to fight all night and a king willing to sleep all day. Oh, how **subtle** the demise. How simple it was to bring one of the greatest kings in biblical history to his knees. It didn't take hordes of demons or years of bad living. *It simply took a willingness to let others fight while he relaxed.* He chose to use the energy of his soul for distraction. Rather than David's energy being spent *attentively* and going off to war, acting like a king, his energy was *distracted*. Rather than his energy being used to battle, it was used to sleep. Rather than his energy being used to lead his men to war, it was used to lead another man's wife to his bed.

Don't ever be lulled into thinking you don't have enough energy to over-come. There's more than enough energy for everyone. If David had enough energy to commit adultery with another man's wife and then plot her hus-band's murder, then he had enough energy to go to war. Actually, after a dili-gent read of the story, I am convinced it took more energy for him to engage in a murderous sex plot than it would have to don a sword and go off to war.

We see here a great deception that will rob you of continued freedom. It's the deception that states, "I don't have enough energy left to fight." Oh, but you do. When you begin to think you are spent and you have no more energy to fight, remember this: the deception resides in the *opinion* that it takes more energy to go to war than to commit adultery in the palace. Are you hoping oth-ers will fight for you? Or are you willing to stop whining and get busy warring?

The best things in life aren't always easy.

Several years ago, I was part of my local fire department. What I gained through my training there was astounding. Often during our time of physi-cal training, I wanted to ring the bell and end the pain and strain of working out. My body would be so fatigued that my mind would be screaming at me, "QUIT! Just quit. You don't have an ounce of energy left." One day during training, I was about to walk off and quit when the chief came over to me and said, "What's wrong, Mark?" "I'm spent," I responded, as sweat was run-ning off me like a waterfall. "You wanna quit?" the chief asked. I held off on answering that critical question. Then he leaned down in my face and said, "Well, if you're not going to quit, get up! This ain't your momma's sandbox."

I made a decision that day. I refused to ever give up. I refused to ever walk off. I refused to ever ring the bell stating I was quitting. After that day of work-outs, I never pondered quitting again. One simple phrase—"This ain't your momma's sandbox"—taught me that the best things in life aren't always easy. It taught me that great accomplishments require great effort and sweat. And it still helps remind me today not to quit when things get tough.

Throughout several years at the fire department, I saw many firemen up and quit during training. Watching this, I learned a valuable lesson. Each fireman who stated he had no more energy to keep going somehow mustered enough energy to get up and quit. Here's the reality: it takes energy to quit. The chief would tell me, "Mark, if someone has the energy to get up and walk away, then he has enough energy to keep going!" Wow! If you have enough energy to get up and quit, then you have enough energy to keep going. What a profound lesson I learned about progress in that firehouse: "Use your energy to move on. Don't use your energy to quit." It never mattered how tired I was or how much my mind was saying, "Quit," I never walked away and quit. I took chief's lesson to heart. I gained some clear insight:

If you have enough energy to quit and walk away, then you have enough energy to keep going and achieve your goal.

It's up to you. It's your choice. If you're tired, confused, frustrated, at wit's end, and ready to quit, then take a moment to reassess yourself. Look at where your energy has been spent this week. Take a moment and make a two-column list with **DISTRACTED ENERGY** on one side and **ATTENTIVE ENERGY** on the other side. Under each heading, I want you to make a list of your thoughts and emotions. Try to pinpoint where the bulk of your energy is being spent. The *distracted energy* side should be filled with all the thoughts, feelings, and emotions that are being used to rehearse, analyze, criticize, and fret over your situation. The *attentive energy* side should be filled with a PLAN of action, what you are doing to better yourself. One side is filled with the actions and energy you are putting forth to tolerate the mess. The other side is filled with the plans and energy of what you are doing to obliterate the mess.

Use whatever energy you have left to dust yourself off and keep going.

Your mind may scream, "I'M DONE!" However, don't use your energy to quit. Use it to dust yourself off and get up. Don't use your energy to file for a divorce; use it to get help. Don't use your energy simmer in bitterness; use it to forgive. Don't use your energy to lash out in anger; use it for kindness. Don't use your energy to criticize others; use it for being thankful. Don't use your energy for gossiping; use it for blessing. Use whatever energy you have left toward achieving a better life and making life better for others. I promise it will be energy well spent. Now fight. Don't give up. Don't quit. I assure you, if you stay in the game and press toward ending your emotional mess, a joyful and content future awaits you.

Don't ever use your last drop of energy to quit.

Chapter 17 Reality Check

1. "You can either spend your energy on chaos or spend your energy on success." Why does it seem harder to live in success than to tolerate chaos?

2. Is most of the energy you spend distracted or attentive?

3. Do you spend the majority of your time rehearsing the problem or working the solution? Why?

4. What are some areas of distracted energy in your life?

5. What are some areas that could use some attentive energy?

6. Distracted energy is spent analyzing the problem. How does analyzing your problem make you feel?

7. Attentive energy works out the solution. Concerning your most pressing situation, how are you staying focused on the solution?

8. Why is it easier to want others to fight for you rather than go to battle yourself?

9. Consider this statement: "If you have enough energy to quit, you have enough energy to keep fighting for your best life ever." Have you ever quit? Why?

10. The big finale: "What are you going to do with the mess in your head?"

CHAPTER 18

Please, Tell Me What to Do!

Years ago, I found myself in a dilemma. I was stuck between a rock and a hard place. I had a decision to make where two paths afforded me an equally good outcome. I stressed over the decision for weeks. I weighed my options. Both sides of the coin fared the same percentage of success. I was stuck. I played the "WHAT IF?" scenarios over and over. I struggled to trust my decision. My emotions kept me awake at night pondering every possibility. As I prayed over the frustration, I finally came to a conclusion, "Why don't I just ask Dad what I should do?" So I picked up the phone and gave my dad a call. I shared all of my frustrations concerning the decision looming over me. He listened intently. I then made my request: "Dad, if you will just tell me what to do, I will do it."

Voilà! I had my answer. He simply *told me what to do*. I simply *did it*. It worked. I never fretted over my decision again. Why? I just needed a shove in the right direction. Once my decision was final, peace came. The moral of my story? I want to help you like my dad helped me. As simple and concise as possible, I will tell you what to do to end the mess in your head. It comes from years of experience—perfected by trial and error. I offer it to you as fatherly advice.

Seventeen Steps To End Your Mess

1. STOP BEING ASHAMED OF YOUR MESS.
    We all have a mess. Welcome to the club. Jesus isn't shocked and He will never abandon you.

2. IGNITE HOPE.
    If you're breathing, there's hope. Bury hopelessness. It will get better.

3. STOP ALL NEGATIVE THINKING.
    Freedom comes by renewing how you think.

4. CONQUER YOUR CHAOS.
    Stop tolerating out-of-control emotions that dictate your mood.

5. STOP "WHAT IFS?"
    You don't have to figure it all out. Trust God instead.

6. TAKE RESPONSIBILITY.
    Don't blame anyone. Denial is deadly. Own it and take a step toward better.

7. FORGIVE YOURSELF.
    You can't go back and get a do-over. Ask for mercy over your mess and expect tomorrow to be a new day.

8. FORGIVE ANYONE WHO HAS EVER BEEN A PART OF YOUR MESS.
    When you forgive those who have wronged you, the mess will no longer control you.

9. KILL EVERY EXCUSE.
    Excuses are never your friend. Consider every excuse a deadly poison.

10. RISK IT.
Break from familiar habits that have created your mess. Don't be scared to be uncomfortable.

11. GET A PLAN.
I'm giving you a plan here. Put it to work. Buy a book, call a friend, attend a class, go to counseling, join a group, enlist a mentor.

12. EMBRACE THE PROCESS.
Freedom doesn't always happen overnight. Don't get discouraged and sidetracked by time spent in the process.

13. MAKE WAR, NOT LOVE.
Out-of-control emotions require a battleground, not a bakery shop. Fight for freedom. Laziness gets you nowhere.

14. CONTROL YOUR MOUTH.
If you can't say something positive, say nothing at all. Your mouth controls your destiny.

15. REFUSE TO QUIT.
It's easy to quit when you feel spent. Use whatever energy you have left to dust yourself off and keep going.

16. READ YOUR BIBLE.
Read the Bible every day. It's the grounds for your strength, your health, your hope, your faith, and your joy. It will give you the ultimate plan for ending your mess.

17. PRAY.
Share your requests with your Heavenly Father. Believe He hears you. Trust He will help you.

Now get busy living your best life ever.

CONCLUSION

Fireflies on the Bedpost

have been asked many times why I titled a book about the mess in our heads *Fireflies on the Bedpost*. It seems odd that my inspiration should come with such a title. The desire to pen this journey came after a long conversation with my oldest daughter. She was away for the summer attending a ministry school almost three thousand miles from home. One morning I took her telephone call and her voice rang out with a certain resolve—a tone I had never before heard in her voice. She began to recount how fear had gripped her during the night, but a vision from God had brought her overwhelming peace. Because I had struggled with wretched fear for years on end, I was intent to hear her story. The moment she began to share with me her vision, I heard God speak to my heart: "I want you to write a book titled *Fireflies on the Bedpost* and teach others how to overcome their emotional messes and how to know My certain peace."

Here is my daughter's vision in her own words.

In July 2012, at age nineteen, I was visiting the beautiful state of California, attending Bethel's School of Worship in Redding. I was lying in bed at my host's home thinking about (or rather, overthinking) the short conversation I had just concluded with Michael, my then-boyfriend (now my husband). He had been feeling sick all day with a stomach bug and couldn't talk long, so we said our good-nights and hung up to chat another time. Immediately, thoughts of death entered my mind.

The thought of my boyfriend dying overwhelmed me. I know it seems extreme. I mean, the stomach bug doesn't exactly scream death, now, does it? But the thought was extreme. It was excruciating! I had never had to struggle with thoughts of dying. Yet, I sincerely feared Michael dying. Here I was, thousands of miles away fearing for his life. I was in an unfamiliar home, questioning whether or not to call my dad to pray over me because I felt I could not handle this overwhelming fear without him. Yet, I felt God lead me to simply close my eyes and rest. Willingly (but still doubting that Michael was going to be OK), I closed my eyes. Immediately, God led me in my mind to a place that I had never been nor seen before. I was lying in a bed in the middle of a jungle. The bed had a canopy and huge bedposts coming up from each corner of the bed frame. I looked up and saw that there were fireflies in jars tied at the top of each bedpost. I then felt Jesus hovering over me. He told me that we had caught the fireflies together earlier that day, and He was giving them to me now as a symbol of His peace. He told me that angels slept above me, and there was nothing to worry about. I began focusing on this picture in my mind: Jesus tying His peace around every corner of my mind. I felt peace. I knew peace. I had peace. I chose peace. Peace was given to me. All fear of death immediately left me, and I fell asleep confident that I was in the hands of the Father.

That night, God transformed the way I dealt with fear. Instead of dwelling on fear, I now choose to dwell on the kingdom of God and what He says about peace. Instead of running from fear, I face it head-on because His peace is unshakable. Instead of taking my every fear to my earthly father and expecting him to pray them away, I lay all my fears now at the foot of my Heavenly Father, and He quickly steadies my heart. He reminds me often of the vision He gave me: fireflies tied to a bedpost bringing the light of His peace.

Therein lies the conclusion of the matter. To find true peace, you are going to have to focus your mind, your situation, your fears, and your emotions on the light of God's glorious character. You are going to have to align yourself with His Fatherhood believing that He is well able to keep you in the middle of the storm. You are going to have to trust Him to lighten your dark world and illuminate His peace over all your fears. In the middle of the fear, in the midst of the chaos, you can simply close your eyes and turn your thoughts to His peace, and let the peace of our Heavenly Father illuminate the darkness of your world.

I summarize all of my advice by pointing you to the character of my Heavenly Father. Your mess can meet His rest. Will you stop tolerating excuses? Will you extinguish all negative thinking? Will you come out from under the spell of your emotions? Will you conquer your chaos? Will you draw your line in the sand? Will you stop trying to figure it all out? Will you regain some hope? Will you take a risk? Will you get a plan? Will you make war? Will you stop fretting over your past and rehearsing your memories? Will you let His mercy take hold on your mess? Will you let a miracle be birthed from your mess? Will you let the Heavenly Father redeem your past and invigorate your future? Will you trust God's Fatherhood? Will you close your eyes and your mind to the fears haunting you and make a clear and distinct choice? Will the voice of Jesus resonate above every emotion? Will you trust His Word? Will you rest in His care? Will you lay all your fears at the feet of your Heavenly Father? Finally, I leave you with one last question:

Will you find His peace in the fireflies on the bedpost?

My prayer is that you do.
—MARK

Made in the USA
Charleston, SC
09 January 2017